HUMAN RELATIONS
for Career Success
Fifth Edition

Steven A. Eggland, Ph.D.
Professor and Chair of Vocational and Adult Education
The University of Nebraska
Lincoln, Nebraska

John W. Williams, Ph.D.
Education and Training Department Head
Time Warner Communications
Englewood, Colorado

JOIN INTERNATIONAL THOMSON PUBLISHING ON THE INTERNET
WWW: http://www.thomson.com
EMAIL: findit@kiosk.thomson.com   A service of I(T)P®

South-Western Educational Publishing
an International Thomson Publishing company I(T)P®

Cincinnati • Albany, NY • Belmont, CA • Bonn • Boston • Detroit • Johannesburg • London • Madrid
Melbourne • Mexico City • New York • Paris • Singapore • Tokyo • Toronto • Washington

Copyright © 1998
by South-Western Educational Publishing
Cincinnati, Ohio

ALL RIGHTS RESERVED

The text of this publication, or any part thereof, may not be reproduced or transmitted in any form or by any means, electronic or mechanical, including photocopying, recording, storage in an information retrieval system, or otherwise, without the prior written permission of the publisher.

I(T)P®

International Thomson Publishing

South-Western Educational Publishing is an ITP Company.
The ITP logo is a registered trademark used herein under License
by South-Western Educational Publishing.

ISBN: 0-538-67931-X

VICE PRESIDENT/DIRECTOR OF PUBLISHING:	PETER MCBRIDE
PROJECT MANAGER:	PENNY SHANK
PRODUCTION COORDINATOR:	TRICIA BOIES
MANUFACTURING COORDINATOR:	KATHY HAMPTON
EDITOR:	ALAN BIONDI
MARKETING MANAGER:	MARK LINTON
DESIGNER:	CAROLE BALACH
INTERNAL ARTWORK:	VICKIE GRANDCHAMP
EDITORIAL SERVICES:	DAVID DEXTER
PROOFREADER:	SUZIE FRANKLIN DEFAZIO
INDEXER:	MAGGIE JARPEY
PREPRESS SERVICES:	CLARINDA CORPORATION

4 5 6 7 8 9 10   C1   04 03 02 01 00
Printed in the United States of America

Preface

The exciting new 5th Edition of *Human Relations for Career Success* is written especially for and about people who are beginning their work life. It is written with the recognition that **getting along with people is the single most important factor affecting chances of success in the workplace.**

The book is based on empirically derived competencies that apply to all employees whether they work for a business, industry, or institution. It is equally appropriate for people working in such diverse organizations as retail stores, hospitals, schools, airlines, law offices, government agencies, or daycare centers. The concepts described in this creative and up-to-date text-workbook will be useful for virtually anyone who works with or for people.

APPROACHABLE TEXT ENGAGES STUDENTS

Like the four very successful previous editions, the 5th Edition of *Human Relations for Career Success* is written in such a way as to be simple to read and easy to understand. It has translated the very sophisticated terminology and concepts of social psychology into everyday language to which students can readily relate. Since the Human Relations movement also contains a great deal of trendy language that tends to lack endurance, this vocabulary, too, is avoided in the text. The book contains a straightforward clearly written formula for success at work.

Once again, each chapter begins with concise and appropriate student **learning** and **attitude goals**.

CHECKPOINT EXERCISES PACE INSTRUCTION

Checkpoint exercises have been added to all of the chapters in this edition. These exercises focus on specific principles and provide brief practice and immediate feedback for the student. All of the checkpoint exercises are designed to assist users of the text-workbook in developing and improving the human relations skills presented in the sections of the chapter they have just covered.

After studying human relations principles and examples, students complete the checkpoint exercises to determine their level of understanding. If desired, they can study the principles again to increase their comprehension.

REVISION EMPHASIZES CUSTOMER SERVICE

Human Relations for Career Success, 5th Edition is significantly reordered and the chapters re-titled so as to focus on customers. More and more, observers and leaders of organizations, business and otherwise, are recognizing and chronicling the importance of customers and service to customers.

♦ **Chapter 1** continues to promote the understanding of human relations as a process and a tool that, when mastered, enables people to succeed in careers. It fosters attitudes including the appreciation and belief that good human relations result in a higher quality of work life.

♦ As the title suggests, **Chapter 2** now is prominently focused on customers. This may be the most important of the revised chapters. Among other things it describes customer's expectations, ways to recognize customers, and provides guidelines for dealing with customers. The chapter also helps the reader develop a positive attitude towards customers and to understand a practical view of the phrase *The Customer is Always Right*.

♦ The Teamwork chapter, **Chapter 3**, continues by developing knowledge and attitudes associated with getting along with co-workers. It describes the rewards of good human relationships with fellow workers and the pitfalls that can be dangerous to good human relationships at work.

♦ **Chapter 4** on organizational effectiveness discusses the topic of human relations from the perspective of an employer. It describes to the reader the importance of getting along with one's employer and cooperating for the greater effectiveness of the organization.

♦ **Chapter 5** highlights the importance of communications as it relates to the development of positive human relationships. The various forms of communications are described with opportunities for practice. Formal and informal communications systems are also discussed. A new element of this chapter encourages students to apply principles of business etiquette to electronic communications strategies.

♦ **Chapter 6** titled "Self Development," emphasizes the importance of knowing and appreciating oneself as a prerequisite to good communications. It describes self-esteem, self-image, and analyses strategies that enable people to acquire self-knowledge.

♦ Finally, **Chapter 7** provides knowledge and suggestions for *Becoming a High Achiever*. It emphasizes the relationship between high achievement and self-confidence.

REALISTIC END-OF-CHAPTER EXPERIENCES DEVELOP CONCEPTS

Throughout the text (at the end of each chapter) are many class activities that, like the rest of the text, are appropriate for all. Many of these activities are brand new for this edition. They are designed to provide realistic and participative experiences that will help develop the concepts brought out in the chapters.

Because of the nature of human relations, most of the activities involve group work and group interaction. The instructor is encouraged to be flexible, creative, and inventive when assigning or directing the student activities. Suggestions for expanded and additional activities are found in the instructor's manual. The text has been specifically designed to cover all of the new basic skills in the human relations realm. In addition, many and various concepts associated with communication at work are presented.

INTERNET ACTIVITIES EXPAND TECHNOLOGY FOCUS

Each chapter in this 5th Edition of *Human Relations for Career Success* includes two creative and dynamic activities in which student's can employ Internet resources. Careful and complete directions for the student and instructor are included with each of these activities and should result in the development of positive human relations skills. Join us on the Internet at:

♦ *http://success.swpco.com*

CHAPTER APPLICATIONS HIGHLIGHT TIMELY TOPICS

Each chapter contains insightful information that provides students with the cognitive and affective social competencies required of people working in interrelating in occupational environments.

SCANS COMPETENCIES AND FOUNDATION SKILLS

The message of the Secretary's Commission on Achieving Necessary Skills (**SCANS**) Report for America 2000, "What Work Requires of Schools" is clear. A much better chance of gaining meaningful employment in the furture will be open to students who develop these skills.

The chart provided in the instructor's manual for this 5th edition of *Human Relations for Career Success* (stock number GK30EX; ISBN: 0-538-67932-8) shows where the SCANS competencies and foundation skills are present within each text-workbook chapter. The SCANS chart supplies an easy reference for instructors to use with students when emphasizing these competencies and foundation skills.

TIMELY END-OF-CHAPTER ACTIVITIES LABELED

The varied types of end-of-chapter activities add value to this text-workbook's content on human relations. Each exericse has important worth and compliments the other exericses. Taken together, the exericses add to the chapters' ability to lead to an understanding and appreciation of human rleations.

To help you identify specific activities, icons are tagged to each of the end-of-chapter activities. These symbols specify the following timely topics:

 **Awareness**

 **Decision-Making**

 Ethics

 Goal-Setting

 Work Quality

 Team-Building

 Understanding Diversity

These topic icons are tagged to their relevant activities both at the end of the chapters and in the table of contents for quick and easy reference.

CORRELATION WITH COMMUNICATION 2000 SERIES PROVIDED

The many different modules in the *Communication 2000* series are innovative applied academics programs that use multimedia technology to present comprehensive communication curricula. Designed specifically to assist students in making the school-to-career transition, *Communication 2000* includes a full line of print and electronic materials presented in a multi-module series.

Using the chart provided in the instructor's manual, you, the instructor, will be able to supplement each chapter in *Human Relations for Career Success*, 5th Edition, with specific lessons from the *Communication 2000* series.

Conversely, users of the *Communication 2000* series will now be able to see at a glance how the different chapters in *Human Relations for Career Success*, 5th Edition, can supplement their work with the different lessons in the series.

TEXT-WORKBOOK MEETS A VARIETY OF CURRICULUM NEEDS

This text-workbook may be used in a great variety of settings over varying lengths of times. It will be absolutely appropriate in virtually any vocational education class. The time consumed could range from seven weeks to a full semester, or it could be a part of another class, or become a class in itself.

Its use will be dependent on the professional instructor's analysis of students needs. However, and for whatever use is made of this publication, it is the authors' sincere wish that it contributes specifically to a pluralistic work force and to the development of greater human relations skills among students preparing for employment and, more generally, to greater tolerance and understanding among people.

REVIEWER SUGGESTIONS MAKE THIS FIFTH EDITION A WINNER

Sincere thanks are extended to the reviewers whose advice and constructive suggestions helped shape this 5th Edition of *Human Relations for Career Success*:

Noamia J. Benefield
North Harris Montgomery County College
Tomball, Texas

Ann Jordan
Great Oaks Institute of Technology and Career Development
Cincinnati, Ohio

Nina Newberry
Tulsa Technology Center
Tulsa, Oklahoma

Jerry O'Bryon
Danville Area Community College
Danville, Illinois

Gail Van Aken-Donnelly
Cherokee High School
Marlton, New Jersey

We are pleased to have this opportunity to share with you the challenge of providing effective instruction. Best wishes for successful human relations in your classes.

Steven A. Eggland
John W. Williams

Contents

1 UNDERSTANDING HUMAN RELATIONS — 1

The Nature of Human Relations for Careers — 2
   Relationships with Customers — 2
   Relationships with Co-Workers — 3
   Relationships with Supervisors or Employers — 3
   Your Relationship with Yourself — 3
Importance of Human Relations — 4
   Beginning of the Human Relations Movement — 4
Check Your Understanding — 5
   The Development of the Human Relations Movement — 6
   Competitive Advantage through People — 8
Success Through Human Relations — 8
   Technical Knowledge — 9
   People Knowledge — 9
Check Your Understanding — 10

Activity 1-1   Learning about Each Other — 11

Activity 1-2   Brainstorming Your Concerns — 13

Activity 1-3   Human Relations with Other Students — 15

Activity 1-4   Why People Get Fired! — 17

2 CUSTOMER FOCUS — 19

Who Is a Customer? — 20
The Importance of Customers — 20
Why Customers Keep Coming Back — 20
   Quality Products — 20
   Exceptional Customer Service — 22
   What Customers Want — 23
Check Your Understanding — 27
   Why Customers Don't Come Back — 27
How to Deal With Any Customer — 29
   Two Simple Guidelines — 30
   Practicing the Guidelines — 30
Is the Customer Always Right? — 31
"It's Business Not Personal" — 32
   Seven Steps for Dealing with Angry or Dissatisfied Customers — 32
Check Your Understanding — 34

Table of Contents

Activity 2-1		Great Moments in Customer Service	35
Activity 2-2		Moments of Truth	37
Activity 2-3		Is the Customer Always Right?	39
Activity 2-4		Who Are They?	41
Activity 2-5		The Card File	43
Activity 2-6		The Angry Customer	45
Activity 2-7		New Employee Orientation	53

3 TEAMWORK   55

Being Accepted	56
Accept Other People's Lifestyles	56
Avoid Incorrect Assumptions	58
Maintain a Good Appearance	58
Develop a Good Attitude	59
Observing the Rules	59
Written Rules	60
Unwritten Rules	60
Carrying Your Own Weight	62
Ask Questions	62
Don't Impose on Others	63
Check Your Understanding	65
Dealing with Conflict	65
Learning or Protecting	65
Developing Tolerance	66
Getting Ahead While Getting Along	69
Why People Want to Get Ahead	69
What People Say and Do to Get Ahead	69
Tips on Getting Ahead while Getting Along	70
Check Your Understanding	72

Activity 3-1		Identifying Written and Unwritten Rules	73
Activity 3-2		Cross-Cultural Business Practices	75
Activity 3-3		Identifying Written and Unwritten Rules	77
Activity 3-4		Asking Questions	79
Activity 3-5		Gripe List	81
Activity 3-6		Getting Ahead while Getting Along	83
Activity 3-7		Flattery	85

4 ORGANIZATIONAL EFFECTIVENESS — 87

- **Understanding an Employer** — 88
  - Employers are Human Beings, Too — 89
  - Success Means Many Things to Employers — 90
- **Employee and Employer Expectations** — 91
  - What an Employee Expects from an Employer — 92
  - What an Employer Expects from an Employee — 94
- **Check Your Understanding** — 97
- **Employers May be Coaches and Mentors** — 97
- **Basic Management Styles of Employers** — 98
  - Authoritarian Management Style — 99
  - Democratic Management Style — 99
  - Laissez-Faire Management Style — 100
- **Quality and Organizational Effectiveness** — 101
  - Follow Quality Processes — 101
  - Fix Processes not People — 101
  - Use Facts and Data to Make Decisions — 102
  - Practice Continuous Improvement — 102
- **What It's Like to be an Employer** — 103
- **Check Your Understanding** — 104

- *Activity 4-1* Interviewing an Employer — 105
- *Activity 4-2* Your Mission Is . . . — 107
- *Activity 4-3* Life Is Not Fair — 109
- *Activity 4-4* Dealing with Authoritarian, Democratic, and Laissez-Faire Employers — 111
- *Activity 4-5* What Leadership Style Would You Choose? — 113
- *Activity 4-6* Quality Management — 115

5 INTERPERSONAL COMMUNICATION — 117

- **Definition of Communication** — 118
- **Barriers to Good Communication and Human Relations** — 119
  - The Problem of Semantics — 119
  - The Problem of *Allness* — 120
  - Misuse of Language — 122
- **Check Your Understanding** — 125
- **The Importance of Good Listening** — 126
  - Why People Don't Listen Well — 126
  - What Good Listening Requires — 128
  - How to Improve Listening Habits — 129

Table of Contents

Official and Unofficial Communication — 130
    Formal Organization for Official Communication — 130
    Informal Organization for Unofficial Communication — 132
Electronic Communications — 136
    Challenges of Non-Face-to-Face Communications — 136
Check Your Understanding — 139

Activity 5-1   Understanding the Definition of Communication — 141

Activity 5-2   Meanings are in People, not in Words — 143

Activity 5-3   Understanding What Allness Is — 145

Activity 5-4   Listening for Emotionally Loaded Words — 147

Activity 5-5   Listening for Facts and Feelings — 149

Activity 5-6   The Wrong Time to Complain — 151

Activity 5-7   Choosing Alternatives to Sexist Language — 153

6 SELF-DEVELOPMENT — 155

Who Are You? — 156
    Your Many Selves — 156
    Putting on Your Best Selves — 156
Check Your Understanding — 163
    Brain Dominance Theory — 164
    What is Important To You? — 164
    The Value System — 165
    Values Relating to Justice — 168
    Managing by Values — 171
Check Your Understanding — 172

Activity 6-1   Riddle of the Sphinx — 173

Activity 6-2   Methods of Revealing Your Many Selves — 175

Activity 6-3   The Johari Window — 177

Activity 6-4   Discussion of the Johari Window — 183

Activity 6-5   Brain Orientation Questionnaire — 185

Activity 6-6   Lookout Mountain — 187

Activity 6-7   A Group Dilemma — 189

Activity 6-8   Values Past, Present, and Future — 191

7 BECOMING A HIGH ACHIEVER — 193

Do You Have a Positive Self-Image? — 194
    How to Develop a Positive Self-Image — 194
    Characteristics of High Achievers — 199

Check Your Understanding — 202

Do You Set Goals in Life? — 203
    Short-Term and Long-Terms Goals — 203
    Goal-Setting Guidelines — 203
    Setting Priorities — 205
    Changing Priorities — 205
    Making Trade-Offs — 205

Activity 7-1   Recognizing Strengths — 207

Activity 7-2   Eliminating Fear — 209

Activity 7-3   The Stress Scale — 211

Activity 7-4   Trust Walk — 213

Activity 7-5   Taking Risks — 215

Activity 7-6   Life Lines — 217

Activity 7-7   Priorities and Trade-Offs — 219

Activity 7-8   Gold in Goals — 221

Index and Photo Credits — 223

1 UNDERSTANDING HUMAN RELATIONS

KNOWLEDGE

After reading this chapter, you will be able to:
- Define **human relations**.
- Describe four aspects of human relations as they relate to customers, co-workers, supervisors and yourself.
- Compare and contrast human relations today and in the early-to-middle 1900s.
- Distinguish between equal employment policies and affirmative-action programs.
- Identify five laws that support equal employment opportunity.
- Identify six common affirmative-action requirements.
- Explain the relationship between technical knowledge and people knowledge.
- Explain the meaning of gaining a competitive advantage through people.
- Describe how good human relations enables a person to succeed in a career.

ATTITUDES

After reading this chapter, you will:
- Appreciate the relationship between technical knowledge and people knowledge.
- Understand that employers want good human relations between employees and themselves.
- Believe that success in a career is dependent on good human relations.
- Believe that practicing good human relations will result in a higher quality of work life.

Learning about human relations as a participant may be the most interesting and exciting activity you've ever experienced. You will soon discover that dealing effectively with people is as simple as understanding a few basic concepts. But it also can be more complex than nuclear physics or computer technology. This book will get you started on a fascinating journey on the way to finding out how to get along with others, while building a successful career.

To understand human relations, first you must know what it is. Then you must know why human relations is important. This beginning chapter helps you understand and appreciate these concepts. It also includes a brief history of the development of human relations. Read and study this material carefully. Complete the Check Your Understanding activities in the chapter and the activities at the end of the chapter. All of these activities will increase your understanding of human relations.

THE NATURE OF HUMAN RELATIONS FOR CAREERS

The term *human relations* refers to *relationships between people*. These relationships can be formal or informal, close or distant, emotional or unemotional. At work many kinds of relationships with different people must be considered. As an employee, for example, you have relationships with customers, with your co-workers, with your supervisors, and with yourself. The business value of these relationships is pictured by the circle diagram in Illustration 1-1. Notice that customers are at the center of the circle. Customers are the most important part of any organization. They are important because without customers businesses would not exist. Without customers there are no jobs, and of course, no careers.

RELATIONSHIPS WITH CUSTOMERS

Following this introductory chapter, the study of Human Relations for Careers begins with customers. The term *customers* usually refers to *people who buy products or services*. Some organizations that sell products or provide a service refer to their customers by different terms. For example, social workers call their customers clients. Below is a short list of occupations and organizations. Fill in the name of the customer synonym used by these groups. Then compare answers with others in your class.

Occupation/Organization	Customer Synonym
Social Worker	*client*
Bus Driver	_____
Hospital	_____
Amusement Park	_____
Computer Technician	_____
School	_____
City Council Member	_____
Entertainer	_____
Lawyer	_____
Internet Service Provider	_____

Most organizations operate under the rule that "the customer is always right." This key human relations rule is not to be taken literally but, rather, in spirit. Although the customer is not *always* right, the customer is always given the benefit of the doubt. The customer must be treated courteously and with respect. When customers are treated this way, the organization and all its employees usually turn out to be successful.

It pays for an organization to develop positive and pleasant human relations with its customers because they will repeatedly return to the business. They will become lifelong customers. If a customer does not return to a business because of poor human relations, the business loses more than one sale. They may lose a lifetime of sales to that customer. Employees of the business can help to build lifelong customers by practicing good human relations. Chapter 2 will help you acquire the skills of getting along well with customers.

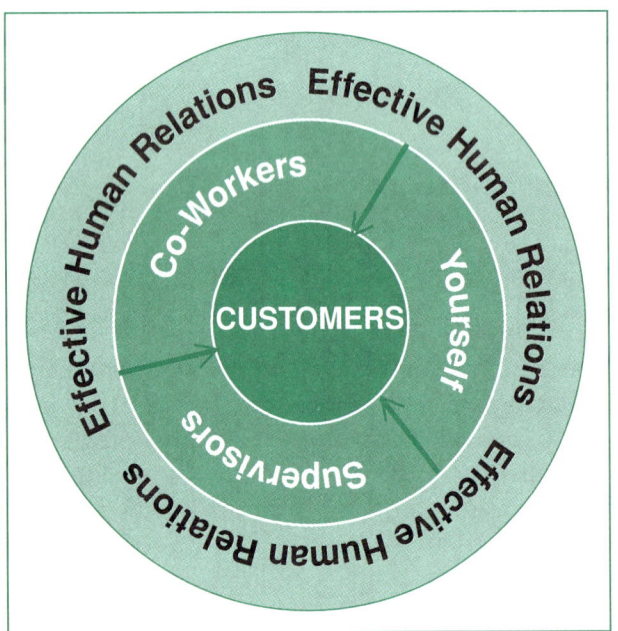

Illustration 1-1
The Business Value of Human Relations

can mean the difference between continued employment and termination. Learning how to better understand the supervisor and what that person expects of you is the key to a good relationship with an employer.

Another way to improve your relationship with your employer is to try to put yourself in your employer's place. Imagining what it would be like to be an employer is a valuable tool. Chapter 4 will provide practice in developing the skill of getting along with employers.

Illustration 1-2
A customer focus is important to business.

RELATIONSHIPS WITH CO-WORKERS

As an employee, you will spend a great deal of time with your co-workers. There are many reasons why it is important to get along with them. Your co-workers may help you or hinder your work. If you learn to get along with them, they will support you and help you get through the rough spots of employment. If you do not get along with them, you can expect very little cooperation from them.

There are several techniques you can master that will improve your relationships with co-workers. Learning to be accepted, carrying your own weight, and understanding written and unwritten rules are just a few of them. Chapter 3 will help you be a team player.

RELATIONSHIPS WITH SUPERVISORS OR EMPLOYERS

The importance of learning to get along with a supervisor or employer can be easily seen. It

YOUR RELATIONSHIP WITH YOURSELF

The study of human relations must include a study of yourself. "That's silly," you might say. "How can I have a relationship with myself?" The answer, of course, is not that you really have a relationship with yourself. Rather, it means that you should get to know and like yourself. You should learn to accept yourself for what you are. This is an important part of your growth and it will enable you to develop plans for self-development.

You can relate positively and successfully to others only if you know yourself and feel good about yourself. If you don't know yourself very well and don't like yourself, this will be very obvious to others. For example, if you are inconsistent, nervous, angry, controlling, self-

Illustration 1-3
Get to know and like yourself.

conscious, and unpredictable, people will have difficulty knowing how to react to you. In other words, they will neither be able to relate to you very well nor have a good relationship with you. Chapter 6 will help you learn to understand the importance of self-development and how it relates to liking yourself. Chapter 7 will show you how to apply self-understanding to becoming a successful high achiever.

IMPORTANCE OF HUMAN RELATIONS

Employers and managers have not always recognized the importance of human relations. During the first third of this century (1900-1930s), they saw little value in human relations. Employees were not treated very well. In those days most employers believed that employees:

1. Had little ambition and tended to shun work.
2. Actually disliked work and, when possible, tried to avoid it.
3. Were only motivated by money.[1]

BEGINNING OF THE HUMAN RELATIONS MOVEMENT

The human relations movement actually began by accident. In the early 1930s, employers were conducting experiments to find ways of increasing the production of goods. One of these experiments, conducted at a Western Electric factory, produced some surprising results. It was this experiment that marked the beginning of the human relations movement.[2]

---

[1]. Douglas McGregor, The Human Side of Enterprise (New York: McGraw-Hill Book Company, 1960), pp. 33-34.

[2]. The Western Electric factory was also referred to as the Hawthorne Plant by the company and its employees. The experiments were also called the Hawthorne Studies. The surprising results became so famous that they were given the name Hawthorne Effect.

The Western Electric Experiment

The purpose of the Western Electric experiment was to see if the amount of lighting in the factory affected the level of production. That is, the experimenters wanted to know if an increase in the amount of lighting would cause an increase in the production of telephone parts. It was hoped, of course, that better lighting would improve the quality and quantity of the production of telephone parts. To test this idea, the experimenters worked with the wiring department of the factory and installed special lights. After the special lights were installed, production of telephone parts increased. The experimenters were naturally pleased with the results. They thought that the improved lighting had improved production.

> *The time is always ripe to do right.*
>
> - Martin Luther King, Jr., in a letter from the Birmingham Jail

A second part of this experiment called for decreasing the amount of lighting. The experimenters thought that if more light improved production, then less light would decrease production. To everyone's surprise, however, the workers continued to produce large amounts of high-quality parts even when the lighting was decreased. And when the lighting was returned to normal, the employees continued to work hard to increase production. As long as the experiment continued, the workers produced greater amounts of high-quality parts. When the experiment ended, the experimenters left the factory in a somewhat confused state because they did not expect these results. A few weeks later, however, production in the wiring department returned to the same level it was *before* the experiment was begun.

Illustration 1-4   Employers' views about employees early in this century.

The Significance of the Western Electric Experiment

The return to normal production had special meaning for the managers of the Western Electric plant. They realized that the experiment itself did not cause the increase in production. Rather, the reason for the increase in production was that the employees in the wiring department received special treatment while the experiment was being conducted. The special treatment they received wasn't anything special by today's standards, but in those days it was. The employees in the experiment got more attention. Managers spoke to them frequently and took more of a personal interest in them and their work. The employees received the special treatment only because they were a part of the experiment. As a result of this special treatment, the employees believed that the owners of the business cared about them. Prior to the experiment, the owners' main interest in the employees was to make sure they worked. After the experiment ended, the employees felt that the owners were no longer interested in them. And that is when their production returned to the old level.

Effects of the Western Electric Experiment on Employers

The news of the Western Electric experiment spread quickly. Alert business owners began to give employees more attention and recognition for their efforts. When employees were asked for their opinions on production problems, employers found that company goals were being reached more easily. The new emphasis at work was now on the employees. Their thoughts and feelings were becoming important. Because of the Western Electric experiment, a new era began in the management of employees. It was called the human relations movement.

CHECK YOUR UNDERSTANDING

To be sure you are reading and learning the key points, fill in the blanks with the missing word or group of words.

1. Understanding human relations can be both very simple and very _____.

2. The term human relations refers to _____ between people.

3. The most important people in a business relationship are _____.

4. Most businesses assume that the customer is always _____.

Illustration 1-5
The human relations movement is working toward eliminating prejudicial employent discrimination.

THE DEVELOPMENT OF THE HUMAN RELATIONS MOVEMENT

The human relations movement advanced slowly. Some years after the Western Electric experiment, employers became aware of the potential of employees. Employers began to recognize that employees were prepared and eager to accept responsibility and wished to share in decision making. More recently, employers started to recognize prejudicial discrimination patterns in the employment of women, minorities, the handicapped, and older people. Actions taken to help these groups of people are creating a work environment free of unfair discrimination.

Meeting the Needs of Employees

During the 1940s and the 1950s, more research similar to the Western Electric experiment was completed. Many activities that are common in organizations today are a result of this research. Such activities include: small-group problem solving, shared decision making, employee recognition programs, quality improvement, and management by objectives.

The immediate results that employees of the 1950s realized were: better working conditions, retirement and benefit plans, and, most important, recognition of employees. Employers began to recognize their employees as a valuable resource for productive ideas.

By the end of the decade of the 1950s, most employers believed that:

1. If working conditions are favorable, most employees will not only accept responsibility, but also seek it.
2. The intellectual potential of the average employee is not being fully utilized by management.
3. When employees are committed to a company, they will exercise self-direction and self-control.

Equal Employment Opportunity and Affirmative Action

Human relations in the 1960s marked the beginning of modern efforts to end prejudicial employment discrimination by treating all employees fairly. These efforts are referred to as *equal employment opportunity* and *affirmative action*.

Equal employment opportunity means that the personnel activities of an organization are conducted without prejudicial discrimination. Personnel activities include:

1. Recruiting and hiring.
2. Working conditions.
3. Salary, benefits, and privileges.
4. Training.
5. Promotions, downgrades, transfers, and layoffs.
6. Terminations.

Any discrimination among employees must result *because of lack of ability* and *not because of* race, color, religion, national origin, sex, age, or physical or mental disability.

In addition to an organization's equal employment policies, the laws of the United States enacted by the federal government include the following acts:

1. *Equal Pay Act (1963)*. This act requires employers to give employees equal pay for equal work.
2. *Civil Rights Act, Title VII (1964)*. Title VII prohibits discrimination on the basis of race, sex, religion, or national origin.
3. *Age Discrimination in Employment Act (1967)*. This act prohibits discrimination in personnel activities because of age.
4. *The Americans with Disabilities Act (1991 and 1996)*. This act is a broad prohibition of discrimination on the basis of disability. The term *disability* means a physical or mental impairment that substantially limits one or more of the major life activities of an individual.
5. *The Family and Medical Leave Act (1993)*. This act provides employees with time off from work to care for a member of the family who becomes ill. It also assures that a parent may have time off from work to care for a newborn child. This includes the mother and/or father and also applies to newborn adopted children.

Affirmative action is literally a positive movement toward a prejudice-free work environment. An organization which states that it is an affirmative-action employer has an ongoing program that guarantees equal opportunity for all employees. It is important to note that affirmative action programs do not require employers to hire unqualified or incompetent people.

Affirmative action programs include many of the following requirements:

1. Active recruiting of qualified candidates for jobs in which imbalances due to race or sex exist.
2. Not tolerating ethnic or sexual harassment or prejudice in the work environment.
3. Requiring all management personnel to conduct ongoing affirmative-action education programs for subordinates.
4. Setting goals and timetables to integrate women and minorities into management positions and nontraditional, non-management positions. (Examples of nontraditional, non-management jobs include: men in clerical jobs and women in outdoor labor jobs.)
5. Entering into contracts with suppliers and vendors whose companies are owned by minorities or women.
6. Designing facilities to make reasonable accommodations for disabled individuals.

COMPETITIVE ADVANTAGE THROUGH PEOPLE

In the last third of the twentieth century, effective human relations has become key business strategy. The strategy centers on gaining a competitive advantage through people. This means an organization wins because of its people. To assure success, organizations have learned that they must promote a diverse work force, encourage healthy life-styles, and recognize that work and family issues overlap.

A diverse work force is a group of employees that includes men and women with variations in race, age, and physical ability. Businesses or organizations often try to maintain a diverse mix of employees. One value of this part of the human relations strategy is in its ability to meet diverse customer needs. It also provides for a more interesting and enlightened work environment.

Healthy employees have good attendance records, positive attitudes, fewer injuries, and they produce higher-quality products. For such reasons, organizations promote physical and mental health and wellness programs. These programs may include help with exercise, advice on diet, and counseling for substance abuse. The Drug-Free Workplace Act of 1988 provides additional incentives for treatment and rehabilitation. The federal law also allows for drug testing of employees.

Some organizations have been slow to accept that work and family issues overlap. A strategy referred to as the *flexible workplace* is gaining widespread acceptance and use. The flexible workplace is an effort to help employees in the areas of:

- Parental leave for newborn children.
- Leaves of absence for elder care (aging or ailing parents).
- Advice and assistance with child care.
- Flexible reporting times for dealing with routine family illness.
- Half days or a few hours off to visit schools or to do community service work.

Other flexible workplace advantages often include opportunities for:

- Regular part-time work—working a regular schedule for less than 40 hours per week.
- Telecommuting—working at home using a computer to communicate with others at work. *Tele* refers to the telephone or telephone lines.
- Secondary work locations—working at a different location than your regular (primary) location.
- Phased retirements—working fewer and fewer hours during the last year(s) of your job.

SUCCESS THROUGH HUMAN RELATIONS

Success in any career requires knowledge and skills. Success just doesn't happen by

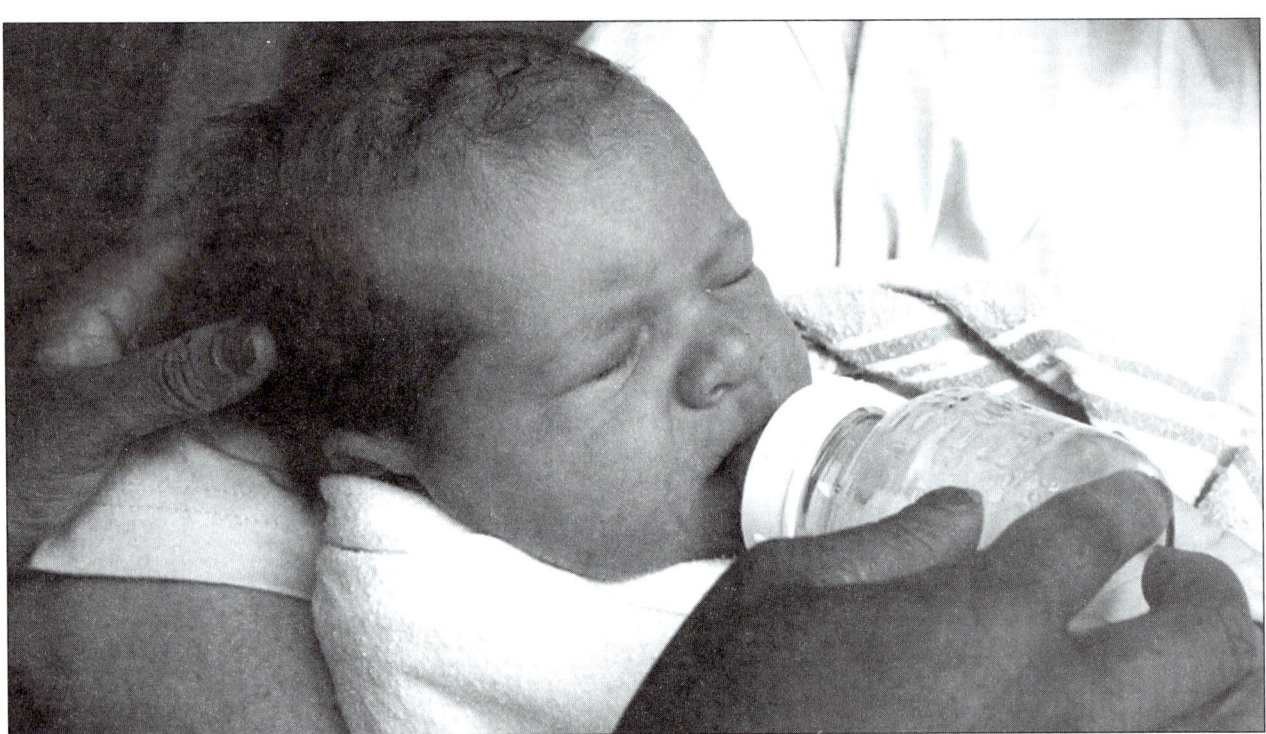

Illustration 1-6
Assistance with daycare is a dimension of the flexible workplace.

chance. You have to make it happen. Everyone gets just about the same number of breaks in life. Those who are ready to take advantage of these breaks are the ones who succeed.

TECHNICAL KNOWLEDGE

Technical knowledge is what you know about the job itself. For example, a lawyer must know the law, a photographer must understand cameras, a chef must know how to cook, and a bus driver must know the route and how to drive a bus. Technical knowledge is often gained by taking classes.

Of course, there are other ways of gaining technical knowledge. For example, you may learn technical skills on the job. You may learn by making mistakes, and you may learn by observing others. The important thing is that, to begin any job, you must have some technical knowledge and skills and know how to apply them.

PEOPLE KNOWLEDGE

To succeed in your career, you must have people knowledge. *People knowledge* means knowing how to get along with customers, co-workers and your employer. People knowledge is human relations. Getting started in a job depends on technical knowledge, but success follows because of your knowledge of human relations. Regardless of your occupation, you must be able to work well with people.

In addition to job success, the increased use of human relations skills by you, your co-workers, and others in the employment environment will lead to much higher quality work life. It is much more pleasant to work in an organization that runs smoothly and has little conflict or strife. When people are getting along with one another, a workplace has more production, fewer mistakes, lower employee turnover, and a general positive feeling of team spirit among its members.

Illustration 1-7
A chef must have technical knowledge to perform the duties assigned to the job.

Working to improve human relations at your place of employment is worthwhile for everyone concerned.

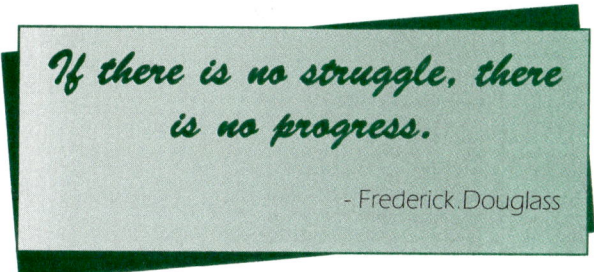

If there is no struggle, there is no progress.

- Frederick Douglass

CHECK YOUR UNDERSTANDING

To be sure you are reading and learning the key points, fill in the blanks with the missing word or group of words.

1. The human relations movement began in the _____.

2. The most significant experiment of the human relations movement took place in a _____ factory.

3. It was the _____ employees received during the experiment that cause their production to improve.

4. _____ means that personnel activities are conducted without discrimination.

5. A positive movement toward a prejudice-free work environment is called _____.

6. Competitive advantage through people means an organization will _____ because of its people.

7. The _____ is an effort to help employees with child care, elder care, and time off for charitable service work.

8. _____ knowledge is what you know about the job itself.

9. _____ knowledge is human relations.

NET WORKING

Join us on the Internet. Check out our Human Relations for Career Success Home Page.

Try some of our special Internet Activities for Chapter 1. Your instructor will give you instructions on which activities would be good for you to complete. Connect with us at:

http://success.swpco.com

CHAPTER 1 ◆ UNDERSTANDING HUMAN RELATIONS 11

Activity 1-1
LEARNING ABOUT EACH OTHER

This activity will help you get to know the people in your class. You may already be acquainted with most or all of them. Nevertheless, by completing this activity, you may learn many things about them that you did not know before.

You need a partner for this activity. Choose someone you don't know very well. Get together with your partner so that the two of you can talk privately. Using the Interview Data Sheet as a guide, take turns interviewing each other. Write out the answer your partner gives to each question. If you do not understand the answer completely, ask your partner to keep talking and explain in more detail.

After you finish interviewing each other, introduce your partner to the class. Using the notes you wrote out during the interview, tell the class about your partner.

Interview Data Sheet

Name of
Interviewee _____

My Name _____

1. What year in school are you? _____

2. Do you work or give volunteer service? Describe some of the things you do that involve other people.

   _____

   _____

   _____

3. Do you have any brothers or sisters? (If older brothers and/or sisters work, where do they work?) What is your birth order in your family?

   _____

   _____

   _____

(Survey continues on page 12)

4. What is your favorite color? favorite word? favorite recording artist?

5. What makes you angry? What makes you laugh?

6. What kind of people do you like? What do you look for in a friend?

7. What is the most meaningful thing that happened to you in the past year?

Activity 1-2
BRAINSTORMING YOUR CONCERNS

The purpose of this two-part activity is to identify some things you want to learn about human relations. After you complete this activity you will know more about the concerns of the members of your class. You will learn that others have different reasons for studying human relations.

Part 1

You have five minutes to complete Part 1 of this activity. During this time period, write out a list of your problems or concerns about getting along with people. For example: Trying to get along with a co-worker who doesn't do his or her share of the work. You may think of a few problems right away, but then you may not think of any problem for two or three minutes. During the last two minutes, you may think of some very important problems. It is important to use the full five minutes! Your teacher will tell you when to begin.

Part 2

Your teacher will give you the next set of instructions for Part 2 of this activity. Use the spaces provided to classify the different concerns of the class. Write each concern or problem under the correct heading.

People Knowledge—Customers

_____
_____
_____
_____
_____
_____
_____

People Knowledge—Co-Workers

_____
_____
_____
_____
_____
_____
_____
_____

People Knowledge—Employers

_____
_____
_____
_____
_____
_____
_____

People Knowledge—Self

_____
_____
_____
_____
_____
_____
_____

CHAPTER 1 ◆ UNDERSTANDING HUMAN RELATIONS   15

Activity 1-3
HUMAN RELATIONS WITH OTHER STUDENTS

NAME

During your study of human relations, you will be required to work closely with other students. To learn how to work successfully with other students, answer the following questions in the spaces provided.

_____
_____
_____

1. How do you tell someone that you disagree with what he or she is saying?

_____
_____
_____
_____
_____

2. What risks are involved in telling someone that you disagree?

_____
_____
_____
_____
_____

3. How do you compliment someone when you like what he or she is saying?

_____
_____
_____

4. Which is easier: to compliment a person or to disagree with a person? Explain your answer.

_____
_____
_____
_____
_____

5. How can you ask a question when you're not sure of how to ask it?

_____
_____
_____
_____
_____

6. What is the definition of a so-called dumb question?

_____
_____
_____(continued next page)

(continued)

_____

_____

_____

7. When you do not understand something, what can you say besides, "I don't understand"?

_____

_____

_____

_____

_____

8. List five qualities that describe your best friend. After you finish, your teacher will give further instructions.

_____

_____

_____

_____

_____

_____

Activity 1-4
WHY PEOPLE GET FIRED!

A University of Michigan study identified the following top ten reasons why people lose their jobs (listed here from least-often to most-often occurring):

10. Problems with co-workers
9. No enthusiasm
8. Lack of interest
7. Lack of initiative
6. Argues with supervisors
5. Lack of skills
4. Tardiness
3. Costly mistakes
2. Can't follow directions
1. Absenteeism

Pick any three of these and describe how they hurt a business.

_____
_____
_____
_____
_____
_____
_____
_____
_____
_____
_____
_____
_____
_____
_____
_____
_____

(More space on opposite side)

2 Customer Focus

Knowledge

After reading this chapter, you will be able to:
- Define the term **customer**.
- Tell why customers return to an organization to buy more goods or services.
- Explain why customers won't come back to an organization to buy goods or services.
- Describe five customer expectations of employees.
- Describe ways to recognize customers and remember their names.
- Give examples of "moments of truth" with customers.
- State two guidelines for dealing with customers.
- State the meaning of the phrase, "The customer is always right."
- Apply seven steps for dealing with angry or dissatisfied customers in a business situation.

Attitudes

After reading this chapter, you will:
- Recognize the importance of retaining customers.
- Believe exceptional customer service helps organizations to attract and keep customers.
- Recognize the value of remembering customers' names and details about them.
- Accept the practical view of the concept, "The customer is always right."
- Accept customers' feelings without arguing.
- Be able to view a transaction through the eyes of a customer.

Customer focus is a term frequently used in business to describe how an organization should concentrate on pleasing customers. An organization focused on its customers knows and understands its customers. In customer-focused organizations, serving customers is the heart of the business.

WHO IS A CUSTOMER?

Most organizations exist to make a profit. That is, they either take or create a good or service, add some value to it, and then sell that good or service for more money than they paid for it. As discussed in Chapter 1, the persons to whom organizations sell their goods or services are generally called customers. A customer is anyone who has a need and who can buy something from an organization to fill that need.

> *If the public don't want to come out to the ballpark, nobody's going to stop them.*
>
> - Yogi Berra

THE IMPORTANCE OF CUSTOMERS

You probably already have a fairly good idea of why customers are important. It has been said that "nothing happens in business until somebody buys something." Without customers, organizations couldn't exist. Customers buy the goods and/or services that organizations offer to the public. Companies must pay the expenses of doing business with the money that the customers spend.

In most cases, there will be some money left over after the company pays the costs of doing business. The money left over becomes the profit of the organization. What the quote also means, then, is that no organization can succeed unless it earns a profit.

So, you can see that the most important element in an organization is its customers because they are the ones who contribute to profits. It literally pays to learn to get along with customers. In fact, you get paid for everything you do for a customer. When you make an effort to get along with customers, they will return time and again to your organization and continue to demand goods or services.

WHY CUSTOMERS KEEP COMING BACK

There are two main reasons why customers patronize, or keep coming back to, any particular organization. These are: (1) quality products and (2) exceptional customer service. Most customers prefer to take their business to establishments that provide both of these. Finding a quality product is often the less difficult. Unfortunately, finding exceptional customer service is unusual. It is so infrequent that people get excited about it and like to tell others about getting truly good service. Let's discuss these two reasons customers patronize an organization. Because the focus here is human relations, after a brief commentary on products, most of the discussion will be devoted to exceptional customer service.

QUALITY PRODUCTS

The first reason why customers keep coming back to an organization is to buy high-quality products. No store, factory, wholesale warehouse, or mail-order company will stay in business long if it produces and/or sells inferior products. The goods that an organization sells to its customers must be of high and lasting quality. The goods must do what the seller says they will do. The goods must be safe and clean. The reputations of some organizations have suffered because they have offered goods of less than top quality to customers. When this happens, customers are disillusioned and buy elsewhere. Employees in organizations should work to see that this doesn't happen. Above all, a customer must be satisfied with the product(s).

Some organizations provide only services. These services are not to be confused with customer service. Service organizations deal in

CHAPTER 2 ◆ CUSTOMER FOCUS 21

Illustration 2-1
There are many varieties of customers.

intangible products, or things that you can't actually touch or keep in your possession as you would, for example, a pair of jeans. A complete list of service organizations would take more pages than this entire book. Some examples of companies that sell services are those that provide entertainment, such as the theater, the bowling alley, and the ball park; those that sell insurance policies to protect people against loss or damage to automobiles or homes; and those that extend credit, such as banks that loan money to people and charge interest for the use of that money.

What are some of the services that are sold or provided by the following organizations? Compare your answers with others in class:

Schools
Health club
Churches
City government
Hotel
Federal government
Cleaning service
United Way
Hair styling shop
American Red Cross

Other organizations provide services to accompany the products that they sell. For example, automobile dealerships repair cars; television stores repair and adjust television sets that they sell; organizations that sell computers often give lessons on how to operate the software programs; department stores offer gift wrapping; furniture stores usually deliver furniture; and pizza restaurants also deliver.

The various services that organizations sell must be of high quality, legal, and fairly priced, and they must provide satisfaction or pleasure. A service must be safe, and it must be provided without discrimination to all who want to buy it.

EXCEPTIONAL CUSTOMER SERVICE

The second reason customers return to an organization is because they received exceptional customer service. All customers have a set of personal expectations when they buy a

Illustration 2-2
Customers come to a business expecting good products, good service, and goodwill.

Illustration 2-3
Customers often see value beyond the purchase price of a product.

product or a service. These expectations are directly related to human relations and how people should be treated. It is this set of expectations that defines customer service. To give customers exceptional service you must learn: what customers want, why customers do not come back, and the meaning of the "moment of truth" with a customer. When you meet a customer's expectations you provide good customer service. When you exceed the expectations you join a small group of very special people. Individuals who provide exceptional customer service have very successful careers.

WHAT CUSTOMERS WANT

Market research is needed to describe customer expectations of products and services of specific organizations. There are, however, general principles that apply to what most customers want and expect from employees when they buy something. These general principles can be classified as: Appearance, Dependability, Responsiveness, Competence, and Personal Attention.

Appearance

The appearance of personnel, equipment and physical facilities are very important to most customers. You might think everyone knows you should be clean and well groomed when you go to work. Many organizations, however, find they must have a dress code for employees. For example, the Denver Colorado Public Schools has a dress code for school bus drivers. This came about because some drivers were wearing torn clothes and generally appeared sloppy. A school board member said it didn't matter how they looked as long as they were good drivers. The Superintendent said that the drivers were ambassadors for the school district and that appearance was important. What do you think?

Appearance of equipment and physical facilities is so important that organizations such as McDonalds, Wendy's Restaurants, and Disneyland hire people to continuously clean and care for the buildings and the grounds. One commercial airline company believes that dirty tray tables in the airplane communicates a sloppy business attitude to passengers. They also worry that these same passengers will think, "If

Illustration 2-4
Whether it's having a repair made or planning an addition to your house, good quality service is important.

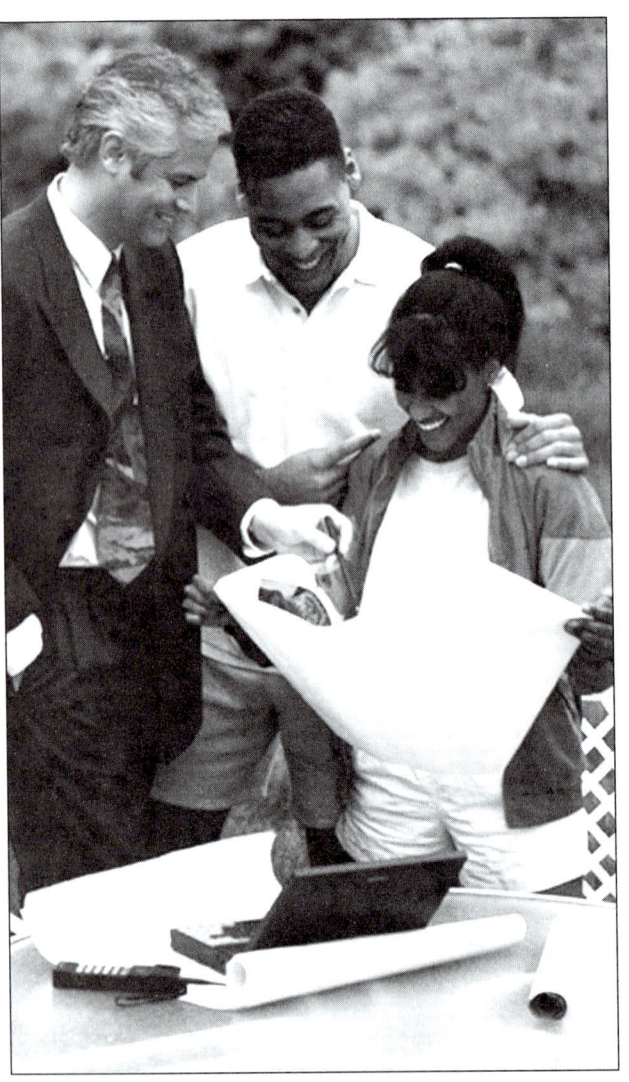

they don't care about a simple thing like clean tray tables, do they care about important things like airplane mechanical maintenance?" Of course, customers would not fly with an airline they believed had poor maintenance procedures. So the appearance of the airplane and the maintenance program of this airline are both first class.

Dependability

Customers expect employees to keep commitments. When you do so you are dependable. When you tell a customer you will do something, you must perform. Rene, for example, operates a photocopy machine and works at the counter for a duplicating service. She must make delivery commitments to customers. Rene provides exceptional customer service by making sure every order is ready as promised. Occasionally the equipment breaks down and a few orders are not ready on time. When this happens, Rene calls the customer in advance of the due date. She explains the problem and gives the customer a new commitment time. In an unusual situation when the equipment broke a second time after Rene had given a new commitment date, Rene took the orders to another duplicating service herself. She made the necessary copies and met her customer commitments.

Responsiveness

Customers expect employees to help them willingly and quickly. Responsive employees look for ways to assist customers. Convenience store clerks are often very good at responding to customers quickly. Al is a good example. He is able to begin adding up the next customer's order while the customer in front writes a check. When the third customer pays with a credit card, Al moves to help the fourth customer while the credit card purchase is processed through the verification system. Al communicates a sense of orderly urgency to the customers.

The Nordstrom Department Store in Seattle, Washington has a unique approach to shoe repair. Most shoe repair businesses try to be responsive by advertising "Shoes repaired while you wait." Nordstrom says, "Shoe repairs instantly while you watch." Nordstrom knows customers don't like to wait! They also know the importance of communicating a responsive attitude to customers.

Solving problems fast is part of being responsive to customers. Customers want fast and easy access to an employee who can fix a problem. If something breaks, "fix it fast" is the motto of organizations that provide exceptional customer service. If you are unable or not authorized to fix the problem, get someone who is—and do it fast!

Competence

Customers expect employees to be knowledgeable about products or services. This knowledge must be communicated to the customer in a courteous and respectful way. Bill, for example, is an experienced hiker and camper. He will only buy equipment from outfitters who know as much or more about the equipment than he knows. When Bill needed to buy new cross-country skis, he drove for two hours to get to a store where he respects the competence of the employees. As an employee, do not try to pretend or fake it when it comes to answering customer questions. If you don't know, get help. Your customer will value your effort to find the answer. This will also build customer trust in what you do say about the product or service.

Personal Attention

Almost everyone likes personal attention. When people remember our birthdays and anniversaries, our hobbies or something else special about ourselves we feel good. The most important aspect of personal attention is remembering a person's name. Dale Carnegie states "The sweetest sound in any language is a person's own name." Customers are no exception. They, too, appreciate recognition. It gives them a certain feeling of importance. People will naturally return as customers to organizations where they are recognized and made to feel welcome. This is a very important fact to understand and to put into practice for anyone who owns or works in an organization.

A popular way to give recognition to customers is simply to remember their names and use those names when greeting them. Try to think back to a time when an employee in a store or other organization greeted you by name. That probably made you feel recognized and accepted. In a small- or medium-sized organization, this is not too difficult to accomplish. In a large organization that serves thousands of people, it can be quite a hard task. It is true that remembering names can be hard. But a few hints will help you remember many names of customers even in a large organization.

Watch for a Person's Name. The first hint is to watch for a person's name. Customers' names will appear on credit cards, driver's licenses, bank checks, business cards, name tags, desk signs, office doors, uniforms or clothing, or in a dozen other places. The trick, then, is to use the name in a greeting ("Hi, Ms. Perez"), in a farewell ("Thanks for stopping at the shop, Frank"), or in a conversation ("This jacket should last for several years, Mrs. Taylor"). Repeating names will help you remember them. But be careful in using a customer's first name. If you do not know the person, it may appear too familiar.

Work Out Word Associations. Another way to help you remember names is to work out word associations. That is, take a person's name and try (privately) to associate it with some unique characteristic of that person. For example, assume that the person's name is Ms. Brownlee and she has long, brown hair. In this case it should be rather easy to remember that the woman with long, brown hair is named Ms. Brownlee. But do be careful to observe when she cuts or tints her hair! You could have fun developing different word associations for people you know and meet.

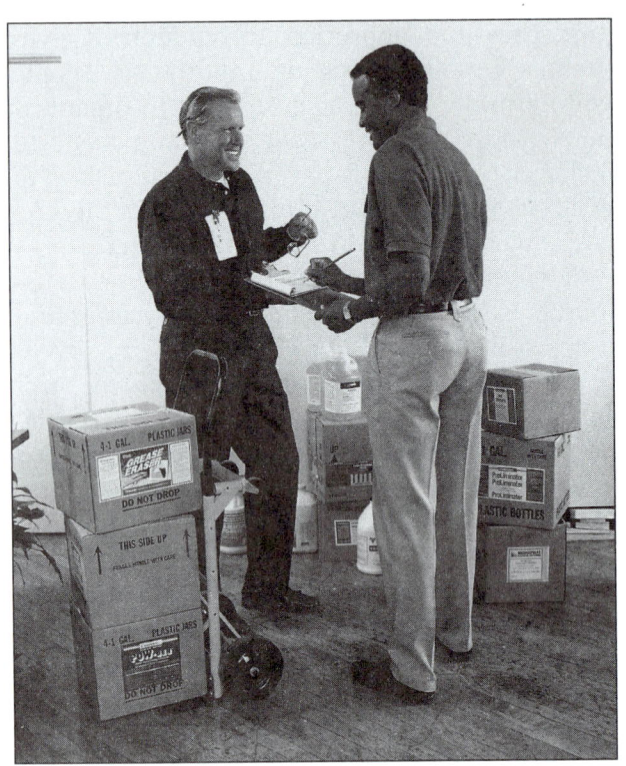

Illustration 2-5
Goodwill may take the form of a positive attitude and personal attention.

Develop a Card File of Customers. Still another way to help you remember customers' names is to start a card file. This is simply a file of 3" X 5" cards or a computer database that contains the customers' names. Looking through this database during your free hours will help you remember names.

The card file may also contain other useful information about your customers. For example, if you are a salesperson in a clothing store, your file would contain each customer's size, favorite colors, taste in fashion, and perhaps even age or occupation. An automobile dealer's database would contain information about customers' cars such as age, model, and make.

It is probably obvious that a file of customers could serve at least two purposes. First, the file will help you remember details about a customer that will help you recognize that customer. In addition to their names, sizes, and brand preferences, customers also appreciate it when you remember the names of their spouses, parents, or children.

The second purpose of a file is to help you sell more goods and services. For instance, if you work in a men's clothing store, you might keep a record of a customer's purchase of new dress suits. A computer database can be set up to send you a message that this customer is six months past his usual date for buying a new suit. The next step would be to telephone the customer or send him a postcard or e-mail, reminding him of some new style or color in a suit that he may prefer. Inviting the customer to come into the store may be just the clincher that will convince him to buy a new suit. When instances like this occur, everyone concerned—the customer, the employer, and the employee—will enjoy the exceptional customer service and improved human relations with one another.

Let us take another example. Elaine was a new-car salesperson who kept a file on former customers. She did this as a service to her customers and as a source of potential sales for her. Elaine knew that it is easier to sell to someone who has already purchased something from you. During slow periods when there were few customers to serve, Elaine made it a habit to call former customers. She would remind them of needed oil changes or of new products that might improve the performance of their cars. Finally, she would ask them if they might like to stop in and look at a new model.

One day Elaine got Mr. Barlow, a former customer, on the line. As Elaine began describing an economy model that she thought might interest him, he responded by saying that he had just been discussing with his wife the pos-

Illustration 2-6
People usually like to be recognized.

sible purchase of a new car. Elaine convinced Mr. Barlow to come and look at the car. Sure enough, Elaine's database system paid off when she sold the car to Mr. Barlow.

CHECK YOUR UNDERSTANDING

To be sure you are reading and learning the key points, fill in the blanks with the missing word or group of words.

1. A customer is _____ and who can _____ from an organization to _____ .

2. "Nothing happens in business until somebody buys something." What does this phrase mean?

_____
_____
_____
_____

3. What is the difference between a product and a service? Give an example of each.

_____
_____
_____
_____

4. What do customers want and expect from employees?

_____
_____
_____
_____

5. List two ways card files can help an employee.

_____
_____
_____

Why Customers Don't Come Back

Organizations that study this question have concluded the following about why customers do not return:

1% die
3% move away
5% are influenced by others to quit
9% leave to the competition
14% are dissatisfied with the product
68% quit because of employee indifference [1]

An indifferent employee is one who does not care about customers.

Karl Albrecht, an expert in customer service research, writes of employee indifference. He found seven ways to get rid of customers:

1. Treat them with apathy.
2. Brush them off.
3. Be cold to them.
4. Treat them condescendingly.
5. Work with them like an unfeeling robot.
6. Stick to the rules.
7. Give them the runaround.[2]

The Moment of Truth

Jan Carlson, the head of Scandinavian Airlines, speaks of "moments of truth" in customer service. A moment of truth occurs when a customer comes in contact with any part of an organization. Contact means much more than helping a customer buy a product or a service. It includes everything the customer sees, hears or smells while doing business with the organization. Moments of truth are the factors that form a customer's opinion of the organization.

Here is an example of how a customer forms an opinion of an organization. Count the moments of truth in this example: Yvonne was shopping for a new blouse. As she walked through the mall, she passed an attractive store window. A blouse she liked was on display in the window. Yvonne entered the store. It had

---

[1]. Jay Conrad Levinson, "Guerrilla Marketing," _Entrepreneur_, April 1996, p. 82.
[2]. Karl Albrecht and Ron Zemke, <u>Service America: Doing Business in the New Economy</u>, 1995 (New York: Warner Books).

Illustration 2-7
Elaine shows a new car to Mr. Barlow.

a musty, moldy smell. A neatly dressed salesclerk was speaking to another employee. The tone of conversation was angry and demanding. The conversation continued as Yvonne looked around the store. She saw dusty shelves and a lot of clothing lint on the new carpet. The cash register counter was cluttered with clothes, clothes hangers, boxes, and paper. The telephone rang and the clerk had to dig through a pile of clothes to find it. Yvonne found the blouse herself. It did not have a price tag on it. Yvonne left the store and continued her shopping at other places in the mall.

If you found at least seven or eight moments of truth, you have a good idea of the meaning of this concept. Do you think Yvonne's opinion of the store changed from the moment she saw the blouse in the window until she decided not to buy it and left the store? Her first impression was favorable. The window display was attractive. Then she entered the store and the moments of truth were more negative than positive. As a result, the store lost a sale. The store may have lost more. Yvonne may not come back and she may tell others of her low opinion of the store.

In summary, customer service is valuable because of the role that it plays in the reputation of the organization and also in the way this reputation is passed on. The reputation of an organization is based at least as much on exceptional customer service as it is based on the quality of goods or services that the organization sells. People tend to remember when their expectations are met. They never forget when their expectations are exceeded. Because exceptional service is so rare, customers tell others about it. This act of passing the word along is often referred to as word-of-mouth advertising. Most organizations realize that this is a very valuable type of advertising because it is free and it is thought to have much credibility or truthfulness. Untold numbers of customers patronize organizations because a friend or a relative referred to it as a good place to do business. Establishing a good reputation through exceptional customer service will surely make them keep coming back.

HOW TO DEAL WITH ANY CUSTOMER

Much could be written about how to deal with all of the different types of customers. Customers may be rich or poor, frugal or spendthrift, young or old. They may be grouchy or happy, bright or confused, set in their ways or willing to try anything new. Or customers may be "just looking." It would be a hopeless task to try to develop a set of guidelines on how to get along and improve your relationships with the many categories of customers that exist. It would probably be more useful to develop one set of guidelines that is appropriate for dealing with any customer.

As a background for developing guidelines, let's review what a customer, or a potential customer, is. A customer is any person who has a need and who can buy something to fill that need. This definition covers a great number of people. A customer may be one who needs glasses, change for a parking meter, a used bicycle, or a pair of pliers. Or a customer may be one who is seeking a friendly face, a gift for a

Illustration 2-8
Customers have many different needs.

grandchild, shelter from the rain, a hot dog, or a fluted gizmo. The point to remember is that customers have many varying characteristics and many different needs.

> *The sweetest sound in any language is your own name.*
>
> - Dale Carnegie

TWO SIMPLE GUIDELINES

The two most important guidelines for dealing with any type of customer are:
1. Learn the customer's need.
2. Try to satisfy the customer's need.

If you remember and practice these guidelines, they will assist you in any kind of situation. To practice these guidelines, however, you will have to adopt a very sensitive and inquisitive style. Furthermore, you will have to work at finding ways to give the customer what he or she really wants. The best way to introduce you to the skill of practicing these guidelines is to provide examples of people who use them.

PRACTICING THE GUIDELINES

Let us take the case of Francisco, an employee in the hardware department of a discount store. He had the responsibility of ordering, stocking, displaying, and selling a full line of hardware in his department. One day, while Francisco was hard at work arranging merchandise, an elderly man walked slowly into the hardware department. Francisco said nothing because his was a self-service department where customers were allowed and encouraged to select the merchandise they wanted to buy. Soon the man, who was looking over several items, asked, "Don't you have any six-inch brass hinges?"

"No," replied Francisco, "we only carry four-inch, brass-plated hinges. But three of them are strong enough for most residential uses."

"I didn't think you'd have them," continued the elderly man. "I haven't seen them in years. I once was a carpenter, and that's the only thing we ever used to hang a door."

"That's interesting," said Francisco. "My father is a carpenter, and I think he uses four-inch hinges all the time. They seem to work all right."

"Oh, yes, they work all right," the man said. "But the bigger brass ones are stronger."

"Are you hanging a door?" asked Francisco.

"No," replied the elderly man. "I was just browsing and thought I'd see if anybody still carried any of the big, old brass hinges. "

"Is there something else I can help you with?"

It is probably obvious to you, just as it was to Francisco, that the elderly man needed someone with whom he could talk. He probably wasn't interested in buying anything. However, there was a chance that, during his browsing, he might have noticed something he needed and bought it. Francisco did a very good job of listening and analyzing the man's need for companionship. He then tried to satisfy the man's need by briefly talking with him and being friendly toward him. By following the guidelines for dealing with any type of customer, Francisco improved his human relations with this potential customer by finding out what the man's needs were and then trying to satisfy them. The elderly man left Francisco's hardware department feeling good. He will probably return one day and buy something from Francisco.

Another example of a person who adopted the two guidelines on dealing with any type of customer was Erin. She was the manager of a small dress shop. One day, as she was taking inventory of some dresses, a customer shyly entered the shop. She looked around nervously and then began to turn toward the door. In a very pleasant voice, Erin said, "How are you today?" Then Erin asked her if there was anything she could do for her. The customer replied, "Well, I don't know. I was sort of wondering if you might be able to help me select a birthday present for my sister."

Illustration 2-9
Francisco attends to a customer who is just browsing.

Erin said, "Why, certainly. Tell me what you can about her size."

"Hmm, I don't know," the customer said.

"How tall is she?" Erin asked.

"She's about 5 feet 4 inches tall. She weighs about 115 pounds, and I think her waist is about 28 inches."

"Now, that gives us something to go on," said Erin. "Don't worry, I'll bet we can find a gift she'll really like."

Erin then went on to pick out several dresses for the customer. She purchased one and left the shop confident and happy. Like Francisco, Erin worked at learning customers' needs and trying to satisfy them. The customer was clearly nervous and uncertain when she entered Erin's shop. Her first need was to be reassured, and her second need was to purchase a gift. Erin did a very good job in this case.

With a little thought and sensitivity and a thorough knowledge of the goods and/or services that your employer provides, you, too, can learn to satisfy customers' needs. The trick is not to make assumptions about people and not to fall into the bad habit of treating all customers the same way. Rather, the successful employee recognizes that every customer is different and has various needs. Then that employee works to satisfy those needs.

IS THE CUSTOMER ALWAYS RIGHT?

You have no doubt heard of the phrase, "The customer is always right." Yet you know that it is not possible for anyone to be right all of the time. Have you ever wondered what this phrase really means?

The idea that the customer is always right is designed to reflect an attitude. That attitude is a good and positive feeling directed toward the customer. It means that the customer's point of view should always be taken into consideration.

Illustration 2-10
Erin is good at learning a customer's needs and trying to satisfy them.

It also means that an employee should never argue with a customer. Rather, an employee should try very hard to see the customer's viewpoint when working to learn his or her needs.

To illustrate this attitude, take the case of the interaction between Sonja, a service station employee, and one of her customers, Erik. He pulled into the station one day and asked her to fill his car with premium gasoline and to check the engine oil. Sonja had just changed the oil and lubricated Erik's car a week ago. She was certain that the oil could not be low so soon. But, rather than argue with Erik, she quickly checked the oil level and found it to be OK.

Even though Sonja knew she was right, she was wise not to argue with Erik. Arguing would have accomplished nothing. In fact, it could have caused Erik to develop bad feelings toward Sonja and the service station. Then, Erik might have decided to do no more business at that station. By not arguing with Erik, no harm was done. And Erik left with his car full of gas, pleased and feeling that he had received value for his money.

"IT'S BUSINESS, NOT PERSONAL"

Like the phrase, "The customer is always right," you may have heard the phrase, "It's business, not personal." Although the original meaning of this second phrase may refer to a different matter, as an employee you should take comfort in it. Remembering this phrase should make you feel better whenever you must deal with difficult customers. The following discussion includes specific actions that can help you deal with angry customers.

SEVEN STEPS FOR DEALING WITH ANGRY OR DISSATIFIED CUSTOMERS

Sometimes a customer enters a store looking concerned or upset. Perhaps that customer is taking back a piece of merchandise that has not proved to be satisfactory. Such a customer may have the feeling that he or she has been cheated in some way by not having received his or her "money's worth." In an effort to get a "fair shake," the customer may use aggression. This means that he or she will appear very angry and demand a refund. The customer may also make threatening, accusing, and downgrading statements about the organization. Sometimes the customer's statements are directed not only at the organization, but also at you, the employee. Here are seven steps for dealing with angry customers.

1. *Agree that the customer has a problem.* Try saying understanding statements such as, "This is unfortunate, it must really upset you"; or simply and in a sincere matter of fact way say, "Yes, that is definitely a problem." An early apology will also help at this point. Why wait until it is all over to apologize? Say something such as, "I am sorry you have been inconvenienced by this." By your acknowledging the problem, and offering an apology, the customer's anger will quickly begin to melt away.
2. *Listen for facts while being attacked.*

Customers sometimes act as if they have a right to be mean and insulting. When they attack, listen selectively. Listen for facts about the problem product or service. This will position you to fix the problem quickly. By your listening and not responding to the attacks, the customer will "vent" his or her anger and be ready to move forward to a resolution of the problem.

3. *Don't take the customer's aggression personally.* Keep cool. Listen some more. Remember the customer did not seek you out personally. You most likely happened to be the person who answered the telephone or greeted the customer. It was a chance occurrence that you got involved. Nonetheless you are involved and you are feeling the brunt of the customer's emotion. Keep saying to yourself, "It's business, not personal."

4. *Ask questions to help get the facts.* The most beneficial questions are What? Where? When? and How? If you ask Who? or Why? questions you may end up blaming a co-worker, or appearing to blame the customer.

5. *Help the customer and the organization win.* This is another way of saying, "Treat the customer as you would like to be treated." Some employees get upset with customers and look for ways to make the customer lose. All too frequently employees decide the angry customer does not deserve help. Then they make excuses for not helping by misusing policy. "Its our policy not to _____ (fill in whatever the customer wants)." Policy is supposed to help you decide; good policy does not tell you what to do. A policy is never a substitute for good judgment. When you get an angry customer, decide immediately that you are going to show the customer how helpful and resourceful you can be.

6. *Promise to take care of it personally.* The customer has some reason for being upset and truly wants help from someone. When you step up and take responsibility for helping to make things right, the customer will see that you are doing your best to help. Say "I will personally take care of this"; or "You can count on me to help fix this problem." Once you commit to taking care of the problem, be sure to follow through.

7. *If you can't fix the problem, get your boss to help.* Sometimes the problem situation requires a supervisor. For example, if you have tried the actions above, and the customer will not be reasonable, swears at you, or threatens legal action, then hand off the customer to a supervisor. The solution the customer needs could be beyond the scope of your authority. Again, in such a situation, refer the problem to a supervisor. If a supervisor is not available, ask the customer to call back or return at a set time. You might also offer to have the supervisor call the customer.

Illustration 2-11
Some customers may become very irate.

In summary, getting along with customers is a skill that is not difficult to learn. Treating each one of them as you would like to be treated, trying to learn their needs, and trying to satisfy those needs will make you a good employee in any organization.

CHECK YOUR UNDERSTANDING

To be sure you are reading and learning the key points, fill in the blanks with the missing word or group of words.

1. What is the biggest reason customers don't come back to buy goods or services from an organization?

_____
_____
_____

2. Explain the meaning of a "moment of truth."

_____
_____
_____

3. List two guidelines for dealing with any type of customer.

_____
_____
_____
_____

4. Is the customer always right? Explain.

_____
_____
_____
_____

5. What is the meaning of, "It's business, not personal"?

_____
_____
_____

NETWORKING

Join us on the Internet. Check out our Human Relations for Career Success Home Page.

Try some of our special Internet Activities for Chapter 2. Your instructor will give you instructions on which activities would be good for you to complete.

Connect with us at:

http://success.swpco.com

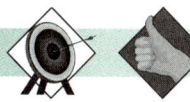

Activity 2-1
GREAT MOMENTS IN CUSTOMER SERVICE

Think of a situation when you were a customer. More specifically, recall the best experience you have had in buying a product or service.

1. Briefly describe the situation.

_____
_____
_____
_____
_____
_____
_____
_____

2. What two or three special things happened to make this your best experience as a customer?

_____
_____
_____
_____
_____
_____
_____
_____
_____
_____
_____

3. What did the salesperson do that you can apply when you are dealing with customers?

_____
_____
_____
_____
_____
_____
_____
_____

4. Why are great moments in customer service so infrequent?

_____
_____
_____
_____
_____
_____
_____
_____
_____
_____
_____

Activity 2-2
MOMENTS OF TRUTH

An example in the chapter related a story about Yvonne shopping for clothes in the mall. In the process of shopping, Yvonne encountered several moments of truth in customer service. In this activity you will be observing moments of truth. Select an organization where you can easily visit and make observations. Any store in a mall is a good observation target. Restaurants (sit near the cash register), public transportation, hair styling shops, churches, and hospitals are also possible sites for your observations.

If you work, make your observations at your place of employment.

Before you start, define "moment of truth" in the space below. Compare your answer with others in your class.

_____
_____
_____
_____
_____
_____

What will you look for when you make your observations? List five specific things you plan to observe:

1. _____
2. _____
3. _____
4. _____
5. _____

After you have completed the observations, answer the following questions.

1. What moments of truth did you observe that surprised you or that you did not expect to observe?

_____
_____
_____
_____
_____
_____
_____
_____
_____
_____

2. How would you rate the organization's "customer focus" (high, medium, low)? Why?

_____
_____
_____
_____
_____
_____
_____
_____

CHAPTER 2 ◆ CUSTOMER FOCUS   39

Activity 2-3
IS THE CUSTOMER ALWAYS RIGHT?

For this activity you will need to identify two organizations: one that sells products and one that sells services. It will be your task to select an owner, a manager, or an assistant manager and ask that person:

"What do you think the phrase 'The customer is always right' really means?"

Take good notes and be prepared to share the answers with the class.

You may contact the organizations in person, by telephone, or on the Internet. When you make contact, be sure to explain that this is for a class project on the importance of human relations with customers.

Use the following format for reporting back to class:

Organization 1

Name of the organization:
_____
_____
_____

Product(s) or Service(s) of the organization:
_____
_____
_____

Name and title of the person contacted:
_____
_____
_____

What the person said:
_____
_____
_____
_____

Organization 2

Name of the organization:
_____
_____
_____

Product(s) or Service(s) of the organization:
_____
_____
_____

Name and title of the person contacted:
_____
_____
_____

What the person said:
_____
_____
_____
_____

Activity 2-4
WHO ARE THEY?

You learned in this chapter that it is important to remember the names of customers. You were also given hints on how to remember names. Below are photographs of six faces with names printed beneath them. In two minutes try to memorize the names of each of these faces. Then turn the page and, without peeking, write as many names as you can remember.

Erik Elridge

Sandra Hahn

Steve Birmingham

Anu Davidson

John Adams

Helen Montoya

Activity 2-4, continued

Write as many names as you can remember in the spaces below:

_____

_____

_____

_____

_____

_____

Activity 2-4, continued

Activity 2-5
THE CARD FILE

Below is a customer card from a card file in an appliance store. Study the card, and then make a list of the points you would make in a telephone call to Ms. Arbuckle.

Remember, the guidelines for dealing with customers are:

1. Learn the customer's need.
2. Try to satisfy the customer's need.

What points would you make in a telephone call to Ms. Arbuckle?

Name: Ms. Ardis Arbuckle
Address: 2121 Vine Street, Lincoln, NE 68508
Telephone: 488-6869
Occupation: University Professor

Appliances Owned	Date Purchased
12A Refrigerator with Ice Maker	1997
14B Countertop Microwave Oven	1996
10X Washer-Dryer Combo	1993
187 Videocassette Recorder	1992
4-Cycle Dishwasher (Portable)	1990

Activity 2-6
THE ANGRY CUSTOMER

Dealing with angry customers may be difficult, but it need not be unpleasant. If you can remember the concept of "It's business, not personal," then you will probably turn an angry customer into a satisfied customer. This activity will help you practice the seven steps for dealing with angry customers.

ROLE-PLAY 1
The Angry Customer

Two volunteers are needed: one to role-play a salesperson and one to play the angry customer. NOTE: Wait until you have created the roles of the customer and the salesperson (see below) before anyone volunteers to play the roles. Half of the class should observe the actions of the salesperson and half should observe the actions of the angry customer. Observation worksheets are included.

A. Create the role of the angry customer by answering the following questions:

- What product is causing a problem?
- What specifically is the customer's concern?
- Does the customer have a receipt?
- What age is the customer?
- What is the financial condition of the customer?
- Is the customer a long-time customer?
- Are there other characteristics you would like to add to the role?

B. Create the role of the salesperson by answering the following questions:

- How long has the person worked as a salesperson?
- What age is the salesperson?
- Assume the salesperson is very good at human relations. What are some of the exceptional customer service characteristics of the salesperson?

The salesperson and the salesperson observers should open the book to the section in this chapter, Seven Steps for Dealing with Angry or Dissatisfied Customers.

Setting: The front of the classroom becomes the place of business. The customer and the salesperson stand and face each other.

Here are the opening lines of the role-play:

Salesperson: Hello, may I help you?

Customer: I hope so. I have a problem . . . (the customer should continue with the problem as created by the class).

Salesperson Observation Worksheet

Rate the actions of the salesperson using the following scale: 1 is low; 10 is the highest level of exceptional customer service.

1. Agrees the customer has a problem.

   1 2 3 4 5 6 7 8 9 10

Comments:

_____

_____

_____

Activity 2-6, continued

2. Listens for facts while being attacked.

  1   2   3   4   5   6   7   8   9   10

Comments:
_____
_____
_____

3. Does not take the customer's aggression personally.

  1   2   3   4   5   6   7   8   9   10

Comments:
_____
_____
_____

4. Asks questions to help get the facts.

  1   2   3   4   5   6   7   8   9   10

Comments:
_____
_____
_____

5. Helps the customer and the organization to win.

  1   2   3   4   5   6   7   8   9   10

Comments:
_____
_____
_____

6. Promises to take care of it personally.

  1   2   3   4   5   6   7   8   9   10

Comments:
_____
_____
_____

7. Refers the problem to a supervisor if appropriate.

   1   2   3   4   5   6   7   8   9   10

Comments:
_____
_____
_____

8. Did the salesperson satisfy the customer?
_____
_____
_____

9. Overall, how did the salesperson perform?
_____
_____
_____

Angry Customer Observation Worksheet

1. How did the customer react when the salesperson agreed that there was a problem?
_____
_____
_____

2. Did the customer seem to calm down as the salesperson listened for the facts?
_____
_____
_____

3. What was the reaction of the customer when the salesperson promised to take care of it personally?
_____
_____
_____

4. Did the customer and the organization win?
_____
_____
_____

Activity 2-6, continued

5. Do you think the customer will come back to the organization to do business?

___

ROLE-PLAY 2
Telephone Complaints

Again, two volunteers are needed. Re-create two new roles of an angry customer and, this time, a customer service person. The setting will be different. The complaint will take place by telephone. NOTE: Wait until you have created the roles of the customer and the customer service person (see below) before anyone volunteers to play the roles. Half of the class should observe the actions of the customer service person and half should observe the actions of the angry customer. Observation worksheets are included.

A. Create the role of the angry customer by answering the following questions:

> What product is causing a problem?
> What specifically is the customer's concern?
> Does the customer have a receipt?
> What age is the customer?
> What is the financial condition of the customer?
> Is the customer a long-time customer?
> Are there other characteristics you would like to add to the role?

B. Create the role of the customer service person by answering the following questions:

> How long has the person worked as a customer service person?
> What age is the customer service person?
> Assume the customer service person is very good at human relations. What are some of the exceptional customer service characteristics of the customer service person?

The customer service person and these observers should open the book to the section in this chapter, Seven Steps for Dealing with Angry or Dissatisfied Customers.

Setting: The two role-players should be seated back-to-back at the front of the room. Because the complaint is by telephone, the role-players should hear but not see each other.

Here are the opening lines of the role-play.

Customer Service: Hello, may I help you?

Customer: I Hope so. I have a problem . . . (the customer should continue with the problem as created by the class).

Customer Service Observation Worksheet

Rate the actions of the customer service person using the following scale: 1 is low; 10 is the highest level of exceptional customer service.

1. Agrees the customer has a problem.

   1   2   3   4   5   6   7   8   9   10

Comments:
_____
_____
_____

2. Listens for facts while being attacked.

   1   2   3   4   5   6   7   8   9   10

Comments:
_____
_____
_____

3. Does not take the customer's aggression personally.

   1   2   3   4   5   6   7   8   9   10

Comments:
_____
_____
_____

4. Asks questions to help get the facts.

   1   2   3   4   5   6   7   8   9   10

Comments:
_____
_____
_____

Activity 2-6, continued

5. Helps the customer and the organization to win.

1   2   3   4   5   6   7   8   9   10

Comments:

_____
_____
_____

6. Promises to take care of it personally.

1   2   3   4   5   6   7   8   9   10

Comments:

_____
_____
_____

7. Refers the problem to a supervisor if appropriate.

1   2   3   4   5   6   7   8   9   10

Comments:

_____
_____
_____

8. Did the customer service person satisfy the customer?

_____
_____
_____

9. Overall, how did the customer service person perform?

_____
_____
_____

Angry Customer Observation Worksheet

1. How did the customer react when the customer service person agreed that there was a problem?

   _____
   _____
   _____

2. Did the customer seem to calm down as the customer service person listened for the facts?

   _____
   _____
   _____

3. What was the reaction of the customer when the salesperson promised to take care of it personally?

   _____
   _____
   _____

4. Did the customer and the organization win?

   _____
   _____
   _____

5. Do you think the customer will come back to the organization to do business?

   _____
   _____
   _____

Activity 2-6, continued

> **Special Questions for the Role-Players**

1. How did seeing or not seeing the other person affect your dealing with him or her?

2. Which would you prefer: to be face-to-face or ear-to-ear?

Activity 2-7
NEW EMPLOYEE ORIENTATION

Work in three-student groups to complete this activity.

You are part of a three-person team working for Network Services Incorporated (NSI). NSI is an Internet Access Provider with its home office in a large city. Your team has been given the responsibility of writing and presenting a part of the customer service section in a new-employee orientation program. New employee orientation is a half-day program that educates new employees about NSI. During orientation, employees get their company ID cards and learn about payroll savings plans, benefits, when and where they get paid, and their role in the company. Your presentation should take about five minutes.

The new employees need to know NSI's views and ideas about the value and importance of customers. Some of your audience will be personally greeting and working with customers. Others will be working with customers on line. Still others will be less directly involved with customers.

What are you going to do with the five minutes allotted to your team? Outline your plan below and on the back of this sheet. Then be ready to present it to the class.

NOTE: Chapter 5, Interpersonal Communication, is about human relations and communications. It will give you tips on how to deal with people through electronic communications.

3 TEAMWORK

KNOWLEDGE

After reading this chapter, you will be able to:

- ✓ Explain the concept of being accepted by co-workers.
- ✓ Compare and contrast written and unwritten rules.
- ✓ Describe the pitfalls of making assumptions.
- ✓ State reasons why people are unwilling to ask questions.
- ✓ Describe common impositions of employees on co-workers.
- ✓ Define **tolerance** and describe ways to increase tolerance of team members.
- ✓ State reasons why people want to get ahead in life.
- ✓ Describe positive and negative aspects of flattery.
- ✓ List guidelines for getting ahead while getting along with co-workers.

ATTITUDES

After reading this chapter, you will:

- ✓ Recognize that the main reason people lose jobs is because they are unable to get along with others at work.
- ✓ Value the ability to accept the differing lifestyles of others.
- ✓ Recognize that appearance and attitude are important aspects of being accepted by co-workers.
- ✓ Value written and unwritten rules.
- ✓ Make an effort to ask questions when trying to find out what is expected.
- ✓ Recognize the importance of the time element in work breaks and in arriving at and leaving from work.
- ✓ Value the ability to show tolerance for others.
- ✓ Value the importance of getting along with co-workers while advancing in a career.

People work for many reasons. Some people work in paid jobs, others work in volunteer organizations, and still others work at home in unpaid jobs. A definition of a *good job* is a job in which you value what you do and you like the people you work with. People who value their work believe that what they do is important. Here, *important* means that the job helps develop or deliver a product or a service.

The second part of the definition of a good job—liking the people you work with or people who are on your team—also implies that you are liked by those same people. Certainly everyone at work does not necessarily like everyone else. This is when human relations becomes important. Your ability to get along with co-workers, whether you like them or not, is often the difference between being unemployed and employed. It amounts to being a good team member.

Those who study reasons why people either leave or lose their jobs have found that there is one main reason. Usually it is not because a worker does not know how to do the job. Instead, the main reason is that many people have a difficult time getting along with their co-workers. As a future employee in any organization, one of the most important skills you can learn is how to get along with other employees. If you can learn how to cooperate with your co-workers, you are well on your way to becoming a good team member and employee in any kind of job.

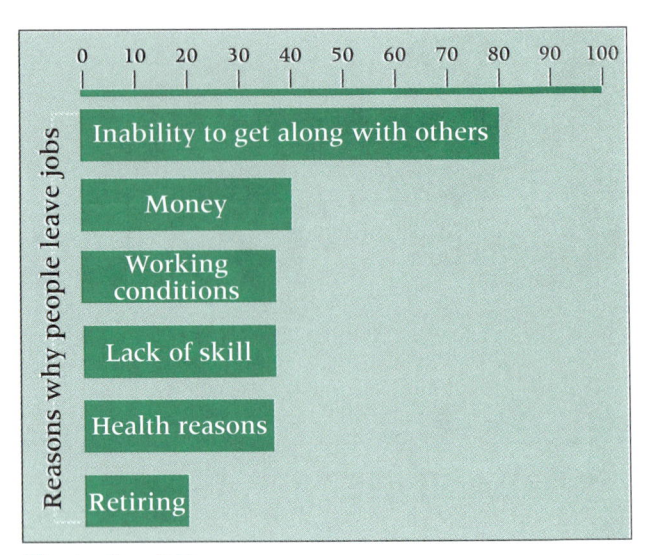

Illustration 3-2
People may give more than one reason for leaving a job, but, by far, the reason most often given is inability to get along with others.

BEING ACCEPTED

Being accepted by others in a job means that they respect you as a co-worker. They listen to you when you talk with them. They recognize you for yourself and welcome you into the organization. Being accepted by others is the first step in getting along in any work environment.

Everyone wants to be accepted by others, and this is especially important to employees. The worker who does not feel part of the team is usually unhappy and not very productive. However, one who does feel accepted by other people at work is more likely to be a happy and satisfied worker. Happy and satisfied workers tend to keep their jobs. They get raises in pay, promotions, and other special recognition from their employers.

Being accepted by co-workers may take some time, but you can reduce this time by using several techniques. Some of the more important techniques are: (1) learning to accept others' lifestyles, (2) trying not to make incorrect assumptions, (3) maintaining a good appearance, and (4) developing a good attitude. If you do these things, others at your place of work will recognize and accept you as a co-worker.

ACCEPT OTHER PEOPLE'S LIFESTYLES

The ways in which people live are called lifestyles. Lifestyles can include people's beliefs, eating habits, housing, education, leisure activities, manner of dressing, and many other daily activities. There are hundreds of different lifestyles, and several of them probably will be represented where you work. The idea, of course, is to respect the way others choose to live and behave. You should never ridicule another's speech, dress, religion, home, eating habits, ideas, or beliefs. It is important to respect another person's right to be different.

Illustration 3-1
People who value their work believe that what they do is important.

Other Cultures

Most often the differing lifestyles that you will likely encounter in the workplace are lifestyles that are associated with different cultures. The United States of America continues to be a land of opportunity accommodating immigrants who want to work and live in our country. These immigrants sometime wear unusual clothing, communicate in special ways, eat unique foods, and have widely varying beliefs and values. Newly immigrated workers are likely to bring these multicultural characteristics to work with them.

In this shrinking world or "global village" we live in, business activities often take place across national borders. In fact, international business is so prominent that none of us, even if we wanted to, is likely to avoid it in some form. When working with people from other cultures it is simply good human relations to be tolerant and accepting of their lifestyles. You might learn to appreciate their foods, enjoy their traditions, admire their clothing and respect their values. In turn, the people from other cultures should try very hard to be tolerant and accepting of our culture.

A good example of a cultural difference in business is the Japanese emphasis on style or process in relation to substance. Most people in the United States are very interested in efficiency in communication and work activity. We are often heard to say "Don't beat around the bush," or "Get to the point." Saying this to a person from almost any Asian culture—especially Japanese—would be insulting. Instead, when dealing with Japanese businesspeople you should be tolerant of and patient with lengthy rituals surrounding introductions and drinking tea, for instance. It may be difficult for some North Americans to understand, but the process of doing business in Japan and with Japanese is as important as the outcome

Even the simplest cultural differences can cause embarrassing situations. When people have difficulty understanding or speaking different languages, the natural tendency is to use hand signals to communicate. Unfortunately, what Americans may think of as international hand signals are not always the same throughout the world For example, the "thumbs up" sign in Israel and Russia is a friendly request for a ride, but in Nigeria and Australia, the thumb

Illustration 3-3
When you are willing to accept others, they will tend to accept you, too.

is an insulting gesture. In Arab countries it means "I am winning." In Spain it can mean allegiance to Basque separatism. Holding your hand out with the palm up and moving the fingers in a wave motion, the "come here" sign, will get the attention of restaurant waiters in Southeast Asia, but it will probably offend them. The OK hand sign is an obscene gesture in Spain, Uruguay, and Brazil. In Japan, it means give me my change in coins.

Do you know any American behavior or language that might unintentionally appear odd or humorous, or in conflict with another culture? Write your example in the space below and be ready to share it with the class.

_____
_____
_____
_____
_____

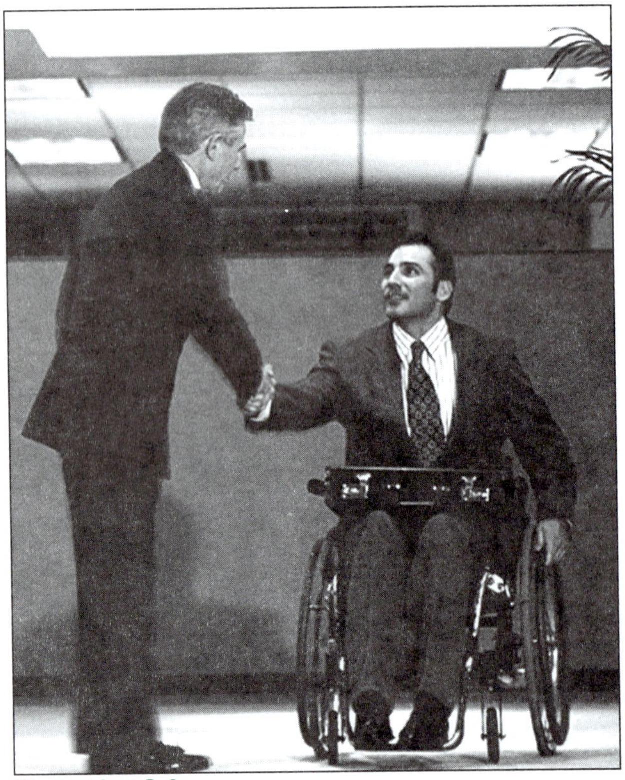

Illustration 3-4
Give some thought to your clothes and grooming before you start a new job.

You may or may not experience these exact situations, however, it is likely that you will meet and work with people from other cultures. When you encounter cultural differences, the surest way to practice good human relations is to be respectful. When you respect others, this quality about you will be quickly noticed. It will help you be accepted in any culture and in any organization. It is also well to remember that accepting other people's lifestyles is usually a two-way street. When you are willing to accept others, they will tend to accept you.

AVOID INCORRECT ASSUMPTIONS

Another technique you can learn to help you become accepted in any organization is closely related to accepting others' lifestyles. It is the art of not making incorrect assumptions about people. Making an incorrect assumption means making a judgment with few, if any, facts. For example, you might assume that a person has difficulty speaking English because that person comes from a foreign country, or you might assume that a person is poor because of his or her manner of dressing. People are often offended by incorrect assumptions made about them. This habit causes poor human relations. Avoiding incorrect assumptions about people can help you find greater acceptance in any organization.

MAINTAIN A GOOD APPEARANCE

Appearance can affect your chances for acceptance at work. Remember that you make a first impression only once. You will improve your ability to make a good impression if you are:

◆ *Alert*—head up, smiling, and looking people in the eye.[1]
◆ *Natural*—using common language when talking with people and not trying to

---
1. Note that good eye contact means giving the other person about the same amount of eye contact that he or she gives you.

impress them with slang or technical terms.
- *Distinct*—speaking clearly without muttering, and using an appropriate voice inflection moderately paced.
- *Pleasant*—using the other person's name while speaking to him or her, ending with a "pleasure to meet you" or "hope to see you again" remark, and delivering these phrases with sincerity.

A good first impression will start you on your way to being accepted.

Give some thought to your clothes and grooming before you start a new job. First, make certain you are clean and neat; that is, teeth brushed, hair combed, body bathed. Also make certain you are appropriately dressed. A good time to learn how to dress for a job is when you are applying for it. Notice how others are dressed for work, and try to wear clothes resembling theirs. Your clothing shouldn't be too dressy or too casual for the job. Whether the assumption is right or wrong, you'll be surprised to find that many people decide to accept or reject others based on their appearance.

Blessed are they that can laugh at themselves, for they shall never cease to be amused.

- Anonymous

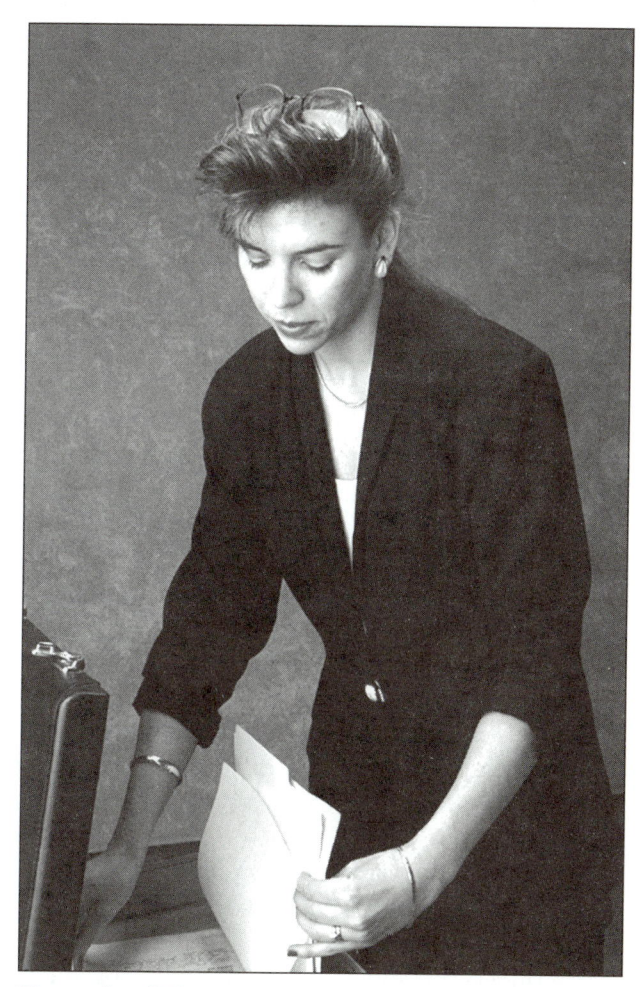

Illustration 3-5
Your clothing shouldn't be too dressy or too casual for the job.

DEVELOP A GOOD ATTITUDE

Perhaps the greatest factor that determines one's acceptance by others in any work environment is attitude. Your work attitude shows how you feel and act about your job and your co-workers. Co-workers are usually more willing to accept a person who has a good attitude.

Having a good attitude can mean many things. It means willingness to work hard and to be ambitious. It means trying to be pleasant to others, as well as trying to be courteous and respectful to those with whom you work. This means that you avoid being a know-it-all or having a chip on your shoulder. Finally, having a good attitude tells people you care about others on your work team.

OBSERVING RULES

Most employers have a set of written rules for employees to follow. In every organization you will also discover that there are unwritten rules that employees are expected to follow. Observing these rules results in better human relations and helps make an organization run more smoothly. By following both written and unwritten rules, you will get along better with your co-workers.

WRITTEN RULES

Many employers prepare handbooks of rules for their employees. Employee handbooks are different from one organization to another, but they contain similar kinds of information. For example, these handbooks will state what the working hours are and what the policies are concerning vacation, sick leave, and work breaks.

Employee handbooks also list rules and suggestions in several other areas. Handbooks may tell how commissions from certain sales are to be divided among employees. They list lunch and dinner hours and rules about use of the employees' lounge. They also state in what parts of the building other activities are permitted.

Organizations in which employees are represented by a labor union have a written set of rules referred to as the contract. The contract is the collective bargaining agreement between the organization and the employees. It is a legal contract and is enforced by law. The contract contains rules and procedures covering such items as these:

- work schedules
- pay
- length of vacations
- days off from work or holidays
- death and disability benefits
- layoff procedures
- grievance procedures

Illustration 3-6
Learn your company's written rules and follow them.

Illustration 3-7
In many organizations people with the most seniority may be allowed to choose their vacation times first.

As a new employee, you will have much greater success getting along with your co-workers if you read and follow carefully your company's handbook for employees.

UNWRITTEN RULES

In almost every organization you will find that unwritten rules exist. Even though these rules are not in writing, you will be expected to follow them if you want to get along with co-workers. How can you find out what these unwritten rules are, and how important they are? Most unwritten rules are based on three factors: (1) the seniority system, (2) territorial rights, and (3) consideration.

The Seniority System

Seniority on the job involves the length of time a person has been employed by an organization. For example, a person who has worked for an organization for ten years would have more seniority than one who has worked there for only two years.

In many organizations people with the most seniority enjoy certain privileges. For example, they may be allowed to take their work breaks first. They may be given the first chance to work overtime for extra pay when there is extra work to be done. Or they may be the first to choose from a scheduled vacation time if there is one.

For unionized employees, most seniority privileges are written into the contract. Some examples of these privileges are listed in the previous section about written rules. In nonunion organizations, the seniority system is usually based on tradition and is not in writing. In either situation—union or nonunion—a healthy respect for the rules of seniority will help you get along with others at work.

Territorial Rights

Territorial rights are similar to seniority, and they are often established over a period of time. These are rights of a person who controls a certain area, or territory. When you are in a territory controlled by another person, you are generally expected to respect the wishes of that person.

For example, in the restaurant business, an unwritten rule involving territorial rights for food servers may be to wait on customers only in designated areas. It is important to know the "territory" of your work situation. Some department stores, for example, may have more strictly defined work areas—a salesperson in the lingerie department may not be welcome in the sportswear department.

Sometimes territorial rights are hard to understand. One way to help understand these rights is to think about some territory that you consider to be your own. For example, you may have your own room, a special chest of drawers, or your special chair. You may become very uncomfortable when someone takes over your own area or areas. Remembering this feeling may help you respect others' territories on the job and may help promote good human relations at work.

Consideration

One of the most important unwritten rules is to be considerate toward those people with whom you work. Being considerate means

Illustration 3-8
It is important to know the "territory" of your work situation.

many things. It can mean sharing the work with someone who suddenly gets very busy. It can mean helping someone lift a heavy box. It could also mean asking permission to use a co-worker's tool. Being considerate of others includes thinking before you act. If you are considerate of others, you will find that you can get along better with them.

CARRYING YOUR OWN WEIGHT

In order to get along with others on a work team, it is important to do your share of the work. In this section you will learn: (1) how to ask questions so that you can find out what is expected of you and (2) what you are expected not to do. To get along with your co-workers, you must carry your own weight.

ASK QUESTIONS

To do a good job, you must know what is expected of you. The best way to learn is to ask questions. Some people do not ask many questions, and as a result they may even do things the wrong way rather than ask questions. The biggest reason some employees don't ask questions is fear—they are afraid to ask! Why are they afraid?

Let's look at some examples. Thelma wasn't sure how to complete a charge sale on the cash register. When a customer wanted to charge the cost of a group's lunch tickets on a credit card, Thelma really got nervous. Because she wanted to do it just right, Thelma asked her supervisor, Ms. Lopez, "Would you help me with this charge sale?" Ms. Lopez answered, "Thelma, you should know that! How many more times do I have to show you how to do this?" Then Ms. Lopez looked at Thelma's customer, frowned, and shook her head. Thelma was embarrassed. She was ridiculed for asking a question. Do you think she will ask Ms. Lopez many more questions?

Another example is Larry, who did not ask questions because he was afraid that other people would think he was not very smart. Larry worried about this because he was not good at spelling. Whenever he had to write an invoice for a sale to a customer, he panicked because he was not sure how to spell some of the items. Rather than ask about the correct spelling, he left some of the spaces blank and misspelled other words. In other sections of the invoice, he tried to cover up by writing so badly that no one, including himself, could read what he wrote. The bookkeeper had to call Larry into the office and ask him about the items on the invoice. When Larry couldn't remember, the bookkeeper had to look up the items by their stock numbers. Larry did not carry his own weight, and the bookkeeper had to carry some of it for him. As a result, Larry had a more difficult time getting along with others. He created extra work for others by being afraid to ask questions.

What can you do if you are afraid to ask questions? Here are some ways to get over the fear of asking questions:

1. *Feel good about yourself before you ask.* If you know you have been working hard to learn your job, then you will feel more comfortable asking questions. Knowing that you are giving 100 percent to the job makes you feel good inside. Then, when you ask a question, it is about something you honestly don't know. Sincerity in asking questions makes other people want to help you.

2. *Ask someone you trust.* Find someone at work whom you like and think you can

Illustration 3-9
Consideration can mean asking permission to use a co-worker's tool or equipment.

Illustration 3-10
Larry would rather misspell than ask or look up the correct spelling.

trust. Tell that person you need to ask questions to learn what you are supposed to do. When you are honest with someone and ask for help, it makes that person feel good. When you ask people for help, you make them feel important and needed.

3. *Face a person who ridicules you—privately.* Do you remember how Thelma felt when she was embarrassed by Ms. Lopez? The best way to clear the air is by a private discussion. Facing up to someone who embarrassed you is very difficult, but the payoff is great. However, actions like this need to be taken privately. As soon as you have the opportunity, talk to the person and explain your double embarrassment: (1) you were embarrassed by your mistake, and (2) you were embarrassed by the way in which you were corrected. Explain that you want and need help, and ask the person to continue giving you help. The best approach is one of sincerity.

DON'T IMPOSE ON OTHERS

Carrying your own weight means more than being good at what you're doing. It also means not imposing on co-workers. Some employees impose on others by (1) calling in sick when they don't feel like working, (2) taking extra-long work breaks, (3) failing to cooperate, and (4) coming to work late and leaving early.

Abusing Sick Leave

Most employers have sick-leave policies described in their employee handbooks. Sick leave is a benefit that allows an employee to be absent from work because of illness. In many cases full-time employees who miss work still get paid for the days they were absent because of illness. Some employees are not ill very often. However, because they use very few sick days, they may feel as if their employer owes them something. As a result, these people may use sick days for one-day vacations. They call in sick when they are well but simply don't want to work that day. This is wrong for two important reasons. First, such employees are cheating their employer. Second, they are also cheating their co-workers. When a worker calls in sick, everyone else on the team has to pitch in and do this absent employee's work.

Extending Work Breaks

In most organizations, work breaks are scheduled. When some employees are in the lounge area during work breaks, others are usually working. One sure and fast way to upset co-workers is to take a long break. If employees extend their work breaks beyond the limit, this upsets the break schedules.

Illustration 3-11
Here is an employee abusing sick leave.

Illustration 3-12
These empoyees are extending their work break and upsetting other employees.

For example, employees who are supposed to get a break at 10:00 don't like to wait until 10:30 just because others have not yet returned from their breaks. Ask yourself, "How would I feel if other workers got longer breaks than I did?" You probably would not be very happy if that situation were reversed. When you work, be considerate and take only the time you're entitled to take on work breaks.

Failing to Cooperate

Doing your share of the work sometimes means helping others on your team. Make every effort to be a team player. When someone has a bad day, make an extra effort to help. Everyone has days or times when he or she does not feel just right. This may happen to you. When it does, your co-workers will also help. Carrying your own weight sometimes means carrying a bit of someone else's.

Being a LIFO (Last In, First Out)

Being the *Last In* to work and the *First one Out* means coming to work at the last possible minute and leaving at the earliest possible time. Being a LIFO can cause poor human relations. Your co-workers and your supervisor may get the feeling that you're not interested in working there. Here is a tip that will make you a better co-worker: Get to work a little early and leave on time. When you come early, it gives you a chance to relax before work and to talk with other employees. This little bit of extra effort can be very important. Getting to work early shows everyone that you like your job and that you are eager to begin working.

Illustration 3-13
Going to work a little early shows everyone that you like your job.

CHECK YOUR UNDERSTANDING

To be sure you are reading and learning the key points, fill in the blanks with the missing word or group of words.

1. What is the biggest reason people leave their jobs?
_____
_____
_____

2. List four techniques for being accepted at work.
_____
_____
_____
_____

3. You make a first impression _____ _____ .

4. Most unwritten rules are based on three factors:
a. _____
b. _____
c. _____

is expected at work may get into a disagreement with other co-workers over who does what work or when and how the work is to be performed. In this situation, the co-worker is new and what the person may attempt to do is different—so conflict develops.

Earlier in this chapter we discussed differences in cultures. When we encounter a new situation where we work with a person of a different culture who behaves differently than we do, conflict may arise. If the way we are treated changes, conflict can develop. When we believe we are treated unfairly, or our ideas are ignored or not valued, conflict may occur. How we react to and deal with conflict is key to successful teamwork. Good team players seek to learn from change and to develop a tolerance for behaviors different from their own.

> *It is not the strongest of the species that survive, not the most intelligent, but the one most responsive to change.*
>
> - Charles Darwin

DEALING WITH CONFLICT

Conflict is a disagreement or dispute between at least two people. It is also possible to have conflict with one person, yourself. This kind of personal, internal conflict is discussed in Chapter 7, Becoming a High Achiever. In this chapter on Teamwork, we will focus on conflict among co-workers.

The source or beginning of conflict is change. When we encounter something new or different, that is, a change, conflict may occur. For example, a new co-worker trying to learn what

LEARNING OR PROTECTING

Reactions to change may be described as learning responses or protecting responses. Learning responses help us understand situations and deal with conflict in helpful ways. Protecting responses tend to avoid conflict or make situations worse. For example, Frank and Alberto, co-workers at a factory that makes boxes for packaging products, got into an argument over a defective product. A new box would not glue together properly. Frank insisted the problem was the production equipment. Alberto argued that the glue was not mixed properly. Frank was responsible for the glue and Alberto was responsible for the equipment. Both tried to protect their work by blaming the other and arguing about who was right.

The problem was finally solved when they shifted from protecting to learning. Alberto asked Frank to explain his thinking so he, Alberto, could learn why the equipment might be at fault. Frank asked Alberto to show and explain why he thought the glue was mixed wrong. Frank wanted to learn if he was mixing the glue improperly.

The best way to deal with conflict is to get into a learning mode as quickly as possible. It only takes one person to get there in order to deal with the conflict in a positive way. Unfortunately, it takes some people hours, or days, or longer to get to a learning mode. Conflict will not be resolved until at least one person gets to the learning mode.

The learning mode need not be complex. Simply agreeing to resolve a conflict by "letting it drop" or forgetting about it can be a reasonable way of dealing with conflict. This usually happens if both sides agree neither will win and continuing the disagreement benefits no one. Following are some characteristics of learning and protecting modes. Read the lists and try to add to them.

Characteristics of Learning Responses

curious
sincere
open
flexible
problem solving
asking
suggesting
thinking of benefits to others and self
welcoming new ideas
seeking to understand

Characteristics of Protecting Responses

anger
hurt
attacking
blaming
silence
sarcasm
either/or thinking
telling others
thinking of self
putting down others
not allowing others to change

Think of recent conflict involving yourself and another person. Did you move into a protecting mode as the conflict began? Did you move to a learning mode so that the conflict could be resolved?

DEVELOPING TOLERANCE

You have learned that getting along with co-workers depends on being accepted, following written and unwritten rules, and carrying your own weight. In this section you will learn about being tolerant of others' habits or mannerisms. You will learn: (1) the meaning of tolerance levels and (2) how to increase your tolerance.

Many good working relationships fail to develop because one person will not tolerate anothers' habits or mannerisms. For example, you may find some of these habits or mannerisms irritating:

◆ Unusual or loud laughter
◆ Bragging
◆ Complaining
◆ Gossiping
◆ Using the same expressions or words too often
◆ Combing hair frequently

Unfortunately, many people do not realize that they have these habits. Furthermore, they may have no idea that others find these habits or mannerisms annoying. If you try to be tolerant of the irritating habits of your co-workers, you will get along with them much better.

Tolerance Levels

The point at which others' habits or mannerisms begin to bother you is called your tolerance level. Your tolerance level constantly changes. In some ways your tolerance level is like a window. On good days the window is open and very little bothers you; you can accommodate a lot. However, on bad days the window is closed, and there is no room inside for any distractions. As you might expect, your tolerance level is high on good days and low on bad ones.

Your tolerance level is very complex. It is affected by things that make you happy and by things that make you sad. Your appearance or even the amount of sleep you had the night before can affect your tolerance level. In the same way, a flat tire on your car, a grumpy friend, or even the weather can influence your level of tolerance. Whereas your appearance and the amount of sleep you have had are matters over which you may have control, you have no control over a grumpy friend, someone throwing a nail in the street, or the weather. Thus, your level of tolerance is determined by two kinds of things: (1) those you can control and (2) those you cannot control.

Illustration 3-15
Do irritating habits bother you?

Increasing Your Tolerance Level

The more tolerant you are, the better you will get along with your co-workers. When you have a high tolerance level, the habits or mannerisms of others don't easily bother you. Before you can increase your tolerance level, however, you must recognize the things you cannot control. These things can be very upsetting, but they happen to everyone and there is not much you can do to change them. If you worry about things you cannot control, you usually lose energy because worrying takes energy. When you lose energy, your tolerance goes down. The best thing you can do is to recognize things you cannot control. Then keep going. Things you have no control over can only shut your tolerance window as tight as you let them.

Once you recognize the things you cannot control, you can increase your tolerance level by exercising power over the things you can control in a situation. You can exercise this power by taking the following steps: (1) separate the irritating behavior from the person, (2) identify your direct and indirect alternatives, and (3) solve the problem by choosing the best direct alternative. These steps will be illustrated by the problem of Don, who had a low tolerance for people who brag.

Separate the Behavior from the Person. Don could not tolerate the way a co-worker, Bob, was always bragging. It was a bad situation because Bob and Don had to work together. Don knew it was important that they get along; however, the situation seemed to be getting worse. Don dreaded each day at work with Bob because he had to listen to Bob brag constantly. Don believed that he had done everything he could to increase his tolerance level, but Bob forced Don's tolerance window closed merely by his presence.

At first Don was ready to quit. However, he decided to take the first step in solving the problem by learning to separate the irritating behav-

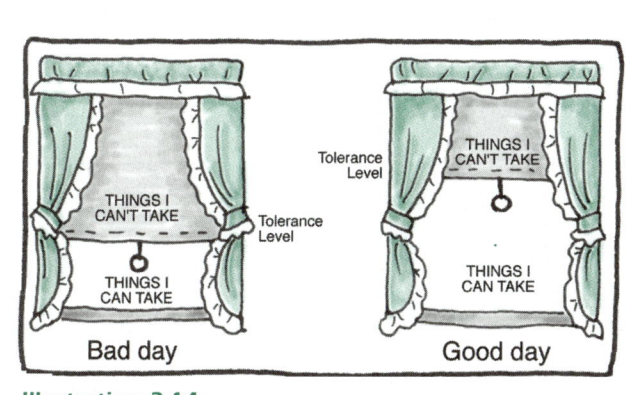

Illustration 3-14
Tolerance Windows

Illustration 3-16
Here is Bob bragging to Don.

ior from the person. Don believed he could like Bob if Bob didn't brag so much. Bragging was the problem, not Bob himself. After all, Bob did a lot of things Don liked. For example, Bob carried his own weight at work. And when Don's car was in the repair shop, it was Bob who would first offer him rides home.

Identify Direct and Indirect Alternatives. Next, Don asked himself, "Now that I have separated the behavior from the person, what do I do?" Don considered asking some of the other employees to do something for him. He thought about asking Lois to talk to Bob, since he thought Lois might subtly explain the problem and ask Bob to stop the bragging. This kind of action, which depends on others for results, is called an indirect alternative. As a general rule, indirect alternatives don't solve problems. Before asking others to do something for you, consider these thoughts: They may not do the task the way you want it done. They may make a halfhearted effort. They may not do the task as quickly as you would like it done.

Don decided it would be better to do something himself. Those things you do for yourself are called direct alternatives. The best way to solve a problem is through direct alternatives because you have the greatest amount of control. Don thought over his direct alternatives. They were:

1. Face Bob and have it out with him.
2. Don't respond to Bob when he brags.
3. Acknowledge Bob's achievement and compliment him on his success.
4. Change the subject when Bob starts to brag.
5. Excuse himself and leave the area when Bob starts to brag.
6. Avoid Bob by staying away from him whenever possible.

Choose the Best Direct Alternative. In the following space, write down what you think is Don's best direct alternative. Then explain your choice.

_____
_____
_____
_____
_____
_____
_____

GETTING AHEAD WHILE GETTING ALONG

Getting ahead means different things to different people. To some people it means more money. To others it means recognition for a job well done. Yet some people see getting ahead as a win-or-lose situation. They think only winners advance, and losers stay behind. You will now explore (1) why people want to get ahead, (2) what people say and do to get ahead, and (3) how you can get ahead while getting along with co-workers on your team.

WHY PEOPLE WANT TO GET AHEAD

There are hundreds of reasons why people work. But most of these reasons are related to three basic factors: (1) money, (2) recognition, and (3) personal satisfaction.

Money

When you have no money, or very little of it, money can be the most important reason to work. But when you have enough to buy most of the things you want, other reasons become more important.

Recognition

Being recognized by your supervisor or co-workers can be the most important reason to work. This was demonstrated by workers at one company. A few hundred assembly-line workers and their supervisors were asked: "What is most important to you?" In their responses, recognition was first; money was second.

An advancement or promotion usually means more responsibility. In some ways an advancement means getting both recognition and money. In order to be promoted, you must be recognized for doing a good job. And when you are promoted, you usually get more money.

Personal Satisfaction

Personal satisfaction is a result of enjoying the work you do. It is a feeling inside of you that is a sense of pride or accomplishment. This special feeling is present most of the time for those who are in a job they like. Some people rarely get this feeling. They are in jobs where the work is just work. They don't dislike the job, nor do they like it. For such individuals, getting ahead at work is unlikely to happen. Most people work at a job at least eight hours a day. Doesn't it make sense to find a job that is pleasant and satisfying?

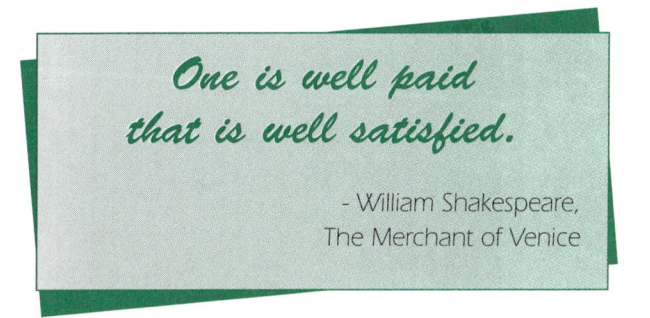

> *One is well paid that is well satisfied.*
>
> - William Shakespeare, The Merchant of Venice

WHAT PEOPLE SAY AND DO TO GET AHEAD

There is a right way and a wrong way to do almost anything. Getting along with co-workers while earning more money, receiving recognition, and achieving personal satisfaction is the right way. Yet some people want recognition so badly that they forget about human relations. Other people simply never learn how to get ahead while getting along. Employees who don't care or never learn about the right way to get ahead can cause problems. Helen's promotion is a case in point.

Helen wanted to become the new assistant manager of a small printing shop. She thought she had a good chance for the promotion because the manager had complimented her several times for her good work. But there were Vincent and Rose, who were her most likely rivals for the job. So, Helen began to make a

Illustration 3-17
There are different reasons for wanting to get ahead.

point of flattering the manager and saying unkind things about Vincent and Rose to other workers. For example, Helen would say: "It seems like Vincent can't get to work on time," or "Why is Rose always making personal telephone calls?" When some of Helen's nasty comments got back to Vincent and Rose, naturally they became upset.

Helen wanted to be a winner. She tried to make Vincent and Rose losers. All her flattering remarks about the manager were made with her own self-interest in mind. Helen may get ahead, but she certainly isn't getting along with her co-workers.

TIPS ON GETTING AHEAD WHILE GETTING ALONG

Getting along with co-workers on your team should be one of your highest priorities. Here are some tips to help you get along while getting ahead:

1. *Accept praise gracefully.* When the manager praises you, look her or him in the eyes and say, "Thank you." Don't put yourself down by saying things such as, "Oh, anybody could have done it." Resist the urge to tell other employees about your personal success. Allow the manager

Illustration 3-17, continued
There are different reasons for wanting to get ahead.

   or a co-worker who might know about your efforts to brag about you.
2. *Share the credit.* Sometimes you receive praise for the efforts of yourself and others. If you do receive credit for doing a job in which others have helped you, share the credit. Accept thanks for your part, but be sure to tell about the efforts of others.
3. *Flatter people sincerely.* Individuals like to hear nice things said about themselves. When you flatter someone, do it because you want to do it. Don't do it because you feel obligated to flatter. To flatter someone because that person can help advance your career is a big mistake.
4. *Don't flaunt special privileges.* As you get ahead, you are given more responsibility. As you assume more responsibility, you will receive some benefits or privileges. You may be given your own desk or you may be assigned special work. When these privileges are given to you, accept them quietly. Don't wave them in front of your co-workers. You have the right to be proud, but resist showing off to your fellow employees.
5. *Let everyone be a winner.* Getting ahead does not mean getting ahead of someone else at any cost. It means getting yourself ahead without putting others down. Putting yourself up by putting others down is a weakness. No one has to be a loser to make another person a winner. If you see your fellow employees as losers, they may try to make you a loser. But if you see them and yourself as winners, you will get along with your fellow team members.

CHECK YOUR UNDERSTANDING

To be sure you are reading and learning the key points, fill in the blanks with the missing word or group of words.

1. Conflict is caused by _____.
2. An example of protecting behavior is _____.
3. List three steps for increasing your tolerance level:

_____
_____
_____
_____

4. Which of the five tips for getting ahead while getting along is most meaningful to you? Why?

_____
_____
_____
_____
_____
_____
_____
_____
_____

NETWORKING

Join us on the Internet. Check out our Human Relations for Career Success Home Page.

Try some of our special Internet Activities on teamwork for Chapter 3. Your instructor will give you instructions on which activities would be good for you to complete.

Connect with us at:

http://success.swpco.com

CHAPTER 3 ◆ TEAMWORK   73

Activity 3-1
IDENTIFYING WRITTEN AND UNWRITTEN RULES

NAME _____

While reading this chapter, you learned that making incorrect assumptions about people can sometimes lead to difficulty. This activity requires you to make some assumptions about the situations in Illustrations 3-18a and 3-18b. Fill in the balloons with some words that you think fit the people in the illustrations. After you have filled in the balloons, below each illustration list the assumptions you made about the situations before you filled in the balloons with words. Then discuss your assumptions with others.

Illustration 3-18a
Making Assumptions

Assumptions:
_____
_____
_____
_____
_____
_____

Activity 3-1, continued

Fill in the balloons with some words that you think fit the people in the illustration. After you have filled in the balloons, list the assumptions you made about the situation before you filled in the balloons with words. Then discuss your assumptions with others.

Illustration 3-18b
Making Assumptions

Assumptions:

_____
_____
_____
_____
_____
_____
_____

Activity 3-2
CROSS-CULTURAL BUSINESS PRACTICES

Asian and American cultures have some uniquely different characteristics. One of the features of the Japanese business protocol is that they are reluctant to say no. North Americans, in contrast, believe a firm, polite no is a sign of strength. No suggests a lack of harmony to the Japanese. And yes doesn't always mean yes in the Japanese culture. The word for yes is <u>hai</u> (pronounced "high"). But it doesn't necessarily mean assent or agreement. It may mean, "Yes, I hear you," or "Yes, I understand you."

Use the spaces below and on the next page to write replies that indicate you are rejecting each offer without saying no.

1. You are offered a third cup of tea.

   _____
   _____
   _____
   _____
   _____

2. "Will you be able to meet with us tomorrow?"

   _____
   _____
   _____
   _____
   _____

3. "Can we ship two dozen of these to you?"

   _____
   _____
   _____
   _____
   _____

Activity 3-2, continued

4. "The price of this item is $10,000. How many would you like?"

Activity 3-3
IDENTIFYING WRITTEN AND UNWRITTEN RULES

Organizations and schools have written and unwritten rules. Either by yourself or as a class, try to write down briefly some of the written and unwritten rules that exist at a place of work or at your school. The first column suggests a type of rule. The next two columns contain space for your examples. Then discuss the questions.

TYPE OF RULES	WRITTEN RULES	UNWRITTEN RULES
Dress Code		
Breaks		
Parking		
Area(s) Off Limits		
Telephone Use		

Other things you can add:

1. Which rules are easier to learn? Why?

Activity 3-3, continued

2. How can the unwritten rules be discovered?

3. Who makes the written rules? The unwritten rules?

4. Are the consequences for violating a written rule more serious than for violating an unwritten rule? Why?

Activity 3-4
ASKING QUESTIONS

Learning to ask questions in a new situation is an important skill. This activity will give you some practice in developing that skill. Follow these directions:

1. Your teacher will select two students in your class to role-play a business situation. One student will take the role of the manager, and another will take the role of a new employee. The new employee may ask for more directions or additional information at any point during the role-playing.

2. The rest of the students in your class should write down the instructions given by the "manager" to the "new employee" in the spaces provided.

Instructions from the Manager:

_____
_____
_____
_____
_____
_____
_____

3. After the role-playing, the person playing the new employee should repeat as many of the instructions as he or she can remember. The new employee may not ask for any new information at this point.

4. The rest of the students should write in the spaces in Table 3-1 what the new employee heard. Did the new employee leave out any instructions (Omissions)? Did the new employee substitute one instruction for another (Substitutions)? Did the new employee confuse any of the instructions given by the manager (Distortions)?

As a class, discuss the following questions:

1. Did the person playing the manager's role give clear instructions?

2. Did the person playing the new employee ask any questions? What were they?

3. Did the new employee understand all of the instructions? If not, what information was left out, substituted, or confused?

4. Why is it important to ask questions if something isn't understood?

Omissions	Substitutions	Distortions
_____	_____	_____
_____	_____	_____
_____	_____	_____
_____	_____	_____
_____	_____	_____
_____	_____	_____

Table 3-1
What the new employee heard

Activity 3-5
GRIPE LIST

This activity may help you let off some steam and at the same time help you learn something about the tolerance of others. Take a pencil and, in the spaces provided, write out your personal "gripe list." Write down all those habits and mannerisms of others that bother you, especially on bad days.

Facial and Bodily Mannerisms

Example: annoying mannerisms, such as absent-mindedly curling one's hair around a finger

_____
_____
_____
_____
_____

Speech and Language

Example: overused words, such as awesome

_____
_____
_____
_____
_____

Voice Sounds and Tones

Example: high-pitched voice

_____
_____
_____
_____
_____
_____

Dress and Appearance

Example: dirty fingernails

_____
_____
_____
_____
_____
_____

1. Place a star next to those mannerisms and habits that bother you even on good days.

2. Compare your list with the lists of others in the class.

3. Discuss tolerance as it relates to your gripe lists.

Activity 3-6
GETTING AHEAD WHILE GETTING ALONG

Read the following case study. Then think about the questions that follow. Answer the questions in the spaces provided.

Case Study

Bonita is president of the student council. Recently, the council sponsored a walkathon for the March of Dimes. Bonita was on vacation with her parents when the council members planned and organized the entire walkathon. When Bonita returned on the day of the walkathon, she immediately took over the responsibility for leading the group. The walkathon was declared a success. The principal of the high school showed how pleased she was by presenting Bonita with a certificate of recognition. Bonita accepted the certificate for herself and then went back to the council members to show it off.

1. Is Bonita correct in assuming that it is her privilege as president of the council to lead the group on the walkathon?

2. Is Bonita behaving appropriately in accepting the certificate for herself? Explain your answer.

Activity 3-6, continued

3. How can Bonita let the rest of the council members be winners, too?

_____
_____
_____
_____
_____

Compare your answers to these questions with the answers given by your classmates.

Activity 3-7
FLATTERY

Read the following article by Sydney J. Harris.[2] Then answer the questions that follow on the next page.

WHY NOT A LITTLE FLATTERY?

Mark Twain once confessed that he could live for three weeks on a compliment, and Mark was not an exceptionally vain man. He was just admitting openly what most of us feel privately.

I never had been one of those high-principled persons who object to flattery because it is "insincere." I don't think there is enough flattery in American life, sincere or insincere. The only kind of flattery to which I have a moral objection is the kind in which the flatterer engages because it will "pay" him. This is bootlicking, and no person of sense or sensibility can help but see through it and despise it.

There is another sort of flattery, however, which is extended not because it gives profit to the donor but because it gives pleasure to the recipient. Most of us need this sort of lift from time to time.

COMPLIMENT THEIR WEAKNESSES

We need it in the most unexpected areas. Good-looking people usually do not require to be complimented. They are well aware of their looks, and may even be bored with them. What they need, most likely, is a compliment on their brains or clothes, or family.

When most of us pay a compliment, we generally pay it to the person's strongest, most obvious point. But to do the greatest good, a compliment should be directed to the person's weakest point or what he thinks is his weakest point.

Twain could not be elated because somebody came up and told him what a fine writer he was; the whole world accepted that fact. But he was radiant if someone complimented an invention he had helped develop.

EINSTEIN, THE FIDDLER

Einstein was a humble man and only shrugged when told how much his genius had revolutionized our ideas of the universe. But a word of flattery about his violin playing (which was mediocre) would bring a sparkle to his eye.

We are a foolish, vain, and doubtful race; even the strongest among us feel weak in some departments. The skillful flatterer is a boon to society, even when he is insincere, so long as his motive is not tainted with self-interest.

---

2. Reprinted with permission, Chicago Sun Times, Copyright © 1991.

Activity 3-7, continued

1. Do you agree with the last sentence in the article? Why or why not?

_____
_____
_____
_____
_____
_____
_____
_____

2. Now your teacher will tell you the name of a person in the class. Write a nice statement about that person on a separate piece of paper. Give the complimentary statement to the teacher. The teacher will give it to the other person. You will also get a complimentary statement from someone.

3. How did you feel about the nice statement written about you? Saying nice things about one another is a good experience, isn't it?

4 ORGANIZATIONAL EFFECTIVENESS

KNOWLEDGE

After reading this chapter, you will be able to:

- Define organizational effectiveness.
- Explain by example what is meant by "Employers are human beings, too."
- List and describe four ways in which employers may experience success.
- Describe the employer and employee sections of an unwritten employment contract.
- Define the following terms or concepts:
  - competence
  - loyalty
  - trustworthiness
  - honesty
  - responsibleness
  - industriousness
- Describe the employer's role in coaching and mentoring.
- Compare and contrast the three basic management styles: authoritarian, democratic, and laissez faire.
- List and describe four principles of quality management.
- Explain why employers must delegate duties and responsibilities.

ATTITUDES

After reading this chapter, you will:

- Recognize that, like employees, employers have human needs.
- Believe that employers should make profits and have a good reputation.
- Value the idea that employees have a responsibility to help employers increase profits and achieve growth in the organization.
- Want to develop traits that will help employees to perform well in their jobs.
- Believe that all management styles can be effective.
- Recognize the importance of the responsibilities employers must assume.

Your organizational effectiveness depends on the degree to which you understand the internal and sometimes invisible activities of the workplace. Internal activities include knowing why an organization exists, knowing what your employer expects of you, and knowing how to get along with your employer on a daily basis.

In some ways, your employer may be the single most important person at work with whom you must develop a good human relationship. Certainly fellow employees, customers, and others in the work environment are important. But without a good understanding between you and your employer, you may not stay employed long enough even to get to know others on the job.

After studying the previous chapter, you are now aware of how important it is for an employee to be able to get along with fellow employees. You learned that many people do not keep their jobs if they are unable to work well with others. In this chapter you will find that it is equally important for employees to work well with their employers or managers. The importance of developing the skill of getting along with one's employer is, of course, obvious. It is the employer who makes decisions about who is hired, who is retained, and who is terminated from employment. If you learn how to develop a good relationship with an employer or manager, you will be able to enjoy a lengthy period of employment.

UNDERSTANDING AN EMPLOYER

Who is an employer? For the sake of simplicity, in our discussion we will refer to any person who is in charge of a group of workers as an employer. This means that an employer could be the owner of a business or the manager of an organization. Although people such as department managers, group leaders, floor supervisors, and so on may not be employers in the strictest sense of the word, they will also be referred to as employers because generally they are in direct charge of a number of employees.

The very nature of an organization demands that someone be in charge and be responsible for its success. This is an inescapable fact. The person in charge has a great deal of responsibility. He or she is usually responsible for such functions as producing goods or services, selling goods or services, handling finances, maintaining good housekeeping and safety, purchasing supplies, and many other activities. Your role as an employee is to carry out your employer's

Illustration 4-1
Your employer can help you understand the inner workings of the organization.

Illustration 4-2
Employers enjoy doing the same things you and I enjoy.

suggestions, ideas, and instructions in relation to the responsibilities that your employer assigns to you. Part of carrying out your own responsibilities includes developing the skill with which to complete your assigned duties. An equally important talent is the ability to get along well with your employer. Getting along means working pleasantly with and for your employer for the overall success of the organization.

EMPLOYERS ARE HUMAN BEINGS, TOO

In order to get along with a person and establish a positive relationship, you learned from the previous chapter that it helps to try to understand that person. This is especially true of learning to get along with an employer. Taking a few minutes to think about your employer's needs will pay big dividends in the form of a good working relationship.

Would it surprise you to discover that there are employers who enjoy doing crossword puzzles, spend every Saturday during the summer at the ballpark, snowboard in the winter, play computer games, write poetry, or read books? There are also employers who create newsletters, practice yoga, cry at weddings, and have spent two years in fourth grade. You should know and remember that employers and managers are human beings, too. They have good days and bad days just like everyone else. They like to receive compliments and, like the rest of us, sometimes have difficulty accepting criticism. They often forget to give praise and sometimes are too quick to criticize. Many of them probably prefer a vacation over work. And, like employees, they appreciate it when everybody carries his or her own weight. Employers are no different from the rest of us. They have likes and dislikes, wants and needs, pleasures and sorrows, and ups and downs. Learning to accept them as people is the first step toward understanding them.

Looking in on one employer might help you better understand the human side of employers. Catherine Christensen is the owner of a large fruit-wholesaling company that supplies retail stores all across the country. She has a large and demanding business and has many employees. As the widowed mother of three children, she is very concerned about their development. She knows it is important to spend a lot of time with her children, and she tries to do that. She has complete responsibility for maintaining a household and small acreage. A painful type of arthritis that flares up for a few days every month is causing her increasing concern. On top of all this, Ms. Christensen also tries to stay active in her garden club because she feels it is important for her to remain socially involved.

If Ms. Christensen's employees knew and remembered these facts about her, they probably would be better able to relate to her. In developing a good relationship with an employer, it helps to remember that every employer has a human side that is often not visible.

SUCCESS MEANS MANY THINGS TO EMPLOYERS

An employer may be managing either a profit-making or a nonprofit organization. Nonprofit organizations include institutions engaged in governmental, educational, religious, and charitable activities. In this chapter, however, we are primarily concerned with employers who manage profit-making organizations. To such employers, success can come in many forms.

Making a Profit

All employers engaged in business want to make a profit. In order to make a profit, businesses must offer goods or services for sale to the public. Making a profit means having money left after all of the costs of doing business have been paid. The costs of doing business include such items as the cost of materials used to manufacture goods, the cost of merchandise that is to be sold or the cost of providing a service, wages and salaries paid to employees, interest paid to banks on borrowed funds, supplies, taxes, and other money paid out by the

Illustration 4-3
Ms. Christensen watches the grading of fruit in her warehouse.

CHAPTER 4 ♦ ORGANIZATIONAL EFFECTIVENESS   91

SUCCESS FORMULA { Sales
Less Costs of Doing Business
Profit

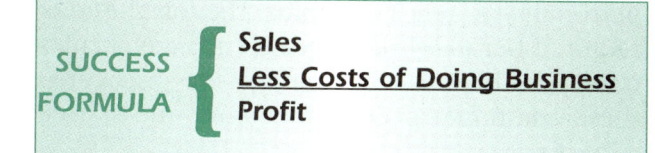

Illustration 4-4
Making a profit means having money (profit) left after the costs of doing business have been paid.

business. All employers engaged in business, therefore, will feel successful if their businesses make a profit.

Achieving Growth of the Business

In addition to profit, many employers work for the growth of their organizations. Growth can mean different things and take many forms. Growth can mean expanding a store or building more stores. It can mean increasing the amount of goods or services that a business sells or offers for sale. Growth might also mean hiring additional employees. In many cases, growth cannot take place unless the company is making a profit. Thus, growth and profits usually spell success to most employers.

Brok's Chicken Barbecue chain provides a good example of a business that is both profitable and growing. While still a student, Charlie Brok opened a small chicken barbecue stand next to the university he was attending. He hired other students to work at the stand while he was attending classes or studying. His barbecued chicken was good. And because his employees worked hard and were very cooperative, Charlie's business prospered and grew. Soon he opened a second stand on the other end of the campus. It, too, became successful. After Charlie graduated, he was able to open up two more chicken barbecue stands in other parts of the city. If the present pattern of producing a good product (chicken barbecue) and maintaining good employer-employee relationships continues, the Brok's Chicken Barbecue chain will surely keep on growing.

Enjoying a Good Reputation

Most employers consider that part of their success includes having a respected reputation in their community. A good reputation is one that is earned over a period of years. It is earned by running a company that is honest and ethical. To gain community respect, the company must provide goods or services of high quality and stand behind them. The company must be fair to its employees. It must respect the environment in which it is located. And it should put some of its profits back into the community in the form of charitable contributions.

Counting Success in Other Ways

Other employers might count success in additional ways. To some, a reputation for offering the finest goods or services in an area may be an important factor. To others, success may mean winning a competitive battle with a similar business down the street or across town. To still others, success might appear in the form of receiving awards from the local Chamber of Commerce for having the most satisfied employees.

EMPLOYEE AND EMPLOYER EXPECTATIONS

Everyone who works has an employment contract. In most hourly paid jobs after one is

Illustration 4-5
An employee filling out an Employee Suggestion Plan form.

16 years of age or older, usually a person first interviews with a personnel manager or the hiring manager. If an offer is not immediate, a verbal telephone offer is frequently the way one gets hired. In most situations, there is no written contract, yet a contract exists at least in our minds: Both you and your employer have expectations about your job. Because unwritten contracts can be the source of many human relations problems, this section focuses on the unwritten employment contract.

WHAT AN EMPLOYEE EXPECTS FROM AN EMPLOYER

The unwritten contract has two main parts: what an employee expects from an employer and what an employer expects from an employee. Let's begin with the employee part of the contract. It contains information about why an employee is working, what is wanted from an employer, and how the work will contribute to long-term employment security. You can be a happier and more productive employee if your part of the contract agreement is clear.

Why Work?

People work for many reasons. Some work for the pleasure that they find in the work; others dislike their jobs and find little if any joy in their work. Some work to be with people; others seek jobs so they can work by themselves. Most people work for money; however, some people volunteer and do not receive money as compensation for their work. For whatever reason, it is essential that people have a clear understanding of why they are working.

For example, Sera, age 16, is looking for a job. Her main reason for wanting to work is to have spending money for clothes and entertainment. Almost any type of work will meet these reasons for working. So Sera took the first job that was offered to her. She quit after one day on the job. It was honest work and a job for which she was qualified. Sera quit because she had unmet expectations about the work. She wanted a job where she could use her outgoing personality to talk to people. The job she took required her to work by herself in a small cubicle-type office. Unfortunately, she discovered these additional expectations after she started working.

Lee was looking for work for very specific reasons. She wanted a part-time job to pay tuition and living expenses until she completed her technical education program. She wanted a job that was near her school or easy to get to riding the city bus. Lee took the first job she was offered that met her criteria.

Both Sera and Lee had unwritten employment expectations. These expectations included specific information about why each wanted to work. Lee was much clearer about why she wanted to work. Her unwritten contract had additional information about working conditions and other things Lee wanted from her employer.

What Do You Want from Your Employer?

What people want from an employer can be divided into two general categories: interpersonal requirements and environmental requirements. Interpersonal requirements deal with how you are treated as a person. These are often invisible or intangible feelings about your boss and your co-workers. Environmental requirements relate to physical working conditions. These are things you can see or touch. They also produce feelings.

Interpersonal Requirements. Everyone wants to be treated fairly and with respect. Everyone wants to be valued as a person who contributes to the success of the organization. And everyone wants recognition for doing a good job. These are the personal requirements most people must have to be happy and successful at work. Almost all unwritten employment contracts contain these items.

Environmental Requirements. Environmental requirements refer to an employee's wants and expectations about working conditions. Some employees seek to work during the day; others prefer night work. Some want work that allows flexible schedules; others prefer a fixed, consistent schedule. Some are concerned about a safe environment where people wear fashionable clothes; others prefer to work with machines and engines that may be hazardous and require special protective clothing. Some people want a job that their friends think is prestigious. Health care is important to some people, so jobs with good medical, dental, and vision benefits are major considerations.

Following is a list of things people expect from their employers. Can you add to the list?

Interpersonal Requirements:

respected and treated fairly
valued as a contributor to the success of the organization
recognized for doing good work

_____

_____

_____

_____

Environmental Requirements:

hours (flexible, fixed, day, night, no weekends)
location
free parking
customer contact/no customer contact
dress code/uniform
health care benefits
vacation/sick days
attractive building
well-equipped employee break room

_____

_____

_____

_____

Illustration 4-6
What do you want from an employer?

How Work Contributes to Long-Term Employment Security

The third item in an unwritten contract deals with employment security. This part of the contract is both an employee expectation and an employer expectation. After we are employed, we usually plan to keep our jobs for a long time. Employers expect us to continually improve on the job so we can be more successful and productive. The challenge is to keep up with changing job requirements. New products, new ways of doing work and changes in customer expectations require new skills and knowledge. If your skills and knowledge are up-to-date, and they are needed by your employer, then you will probably remain employed. It is your responsibility to keep your skills current. Here are three strategies to develop job skills continually once you are employed:

1. *Learn at the speed of change.* Jim is a data specialist. His job is to prepare graphs, charts and other technical information. He uses a computer and software programs that make the graphs and charts. To keep up-to-date, Jim continually learns new features and techniques on the software he uses. He develops shortcuts and ways to improve his speed and accuracy. When the software program is upgraded, Jim quickly learns the additional features and capabilities of the program. When a completely new graphics software package was purchased by the company, Jim was one of the first to volunteer to learn how to run the software. Jim is a good team player—after learning the new software, he enjoys teaching others how to use it.

2. *Learn many functions.* Wanda is an employee of a copy and duplicating service. Her job is to make photocopies of documents. The shop has four different types of copiers. After Wanda learned how to operate one copier very well, she asked her employer if she could learn to operate other more complex copiers. Wanda eventually learned to operate all the copiers in the shop. She also learned how to work directly with customers. Over a period of time, Wanda learned to perform almost every job function in the entire shop. By doing so, Wanda succeeds in making herself valuable to her employer.

3. *Learn future skills.* Chin works as a cable TV installer. He has a career path in mind for himself: to be able to work with satellite systems. To do this, Chin studies television technology in an on-the-job training program and through correspondence courses. Chin doesn't know the exact satellite systems of the future. He does know that satellites are a part of the future. He plans to learn the basic satellite technology and be ready to learn the specifics as they are developed.

WHAT AN EMPLOYER EXPECTS FROM AN EMPLOYEE

The second part of the employment contract includes an employer's expectations of employees. Remember, the contract is usually not in writing, but it is just as important as a written contract.

Employers expect employees to work together for the success of the organization. Some objectives for this success, which were discussed earlier in this chapter, include: making a profit, growing the business, and earning a good reputation. To achieve these objectives, your employer expects you to have or develop certain desirable business traits. These traits have withstood the test of time and have proven to be vital to successful organizations. The traits include: competence, loyalty, trustworthiness, honesty, responsibleness, and industriousness.

> *The only place where success comes before work is in the dictionary.*
>
> – Vidal Sassoon

Competence

An employer expects employees to be competent. This means that employees are expected to know what they are supposed to do and how they should perform their jobs. It is assumed, of course, that employees have had training or preparation for the jobs they were hired to perform. Many would-be employees begin to develop competence when they enroll in vocational or career education classes while still at school. As a rule, competent employees get along well with their employers.

Loyalty

One owner of a company used to say to employees, "If there is something you don't like about our company, please tell us. And if there is something you like about us, please tell others." This employer was really saying that, in return for salary and benefits, the firm expected loyalty from its employees.

Loyalty to a company means going to your supervisor with any problem or complaint that may arise. Part of your supervisor's job is to handle employee problems. Employers prefer to solve their own problems rather than have dissatisfied employees complain about their work to outsiders. In the same manner, employers do not want their employees to criticize the goods or services sold by the company to others outside the company.

Loyalty to a company also means telling outsiders about the fine products or services that your company sells. For example, let us take the case of Leslie, a high school student and part-time employee in a bicycle sales and service shop. One of the benefits of working for ACE Bicycle Company was the privilege of buying a bicycle for 50 percent off the selling price. After saving enough money, Leslie bought a gleaming ACE mountain bike. It was everything one could want in a new bike. Leslie was very proud of it. She spent a lot of time telling her friends and others what excellent products ACE sold. As a result, many people she knew came into the store and bought bicycles. Of course, this made Leslie's employer very happy.

Trustworthiness

There are many cases when an employer or supervisor is able to place an employee in a

Illustration 4-7
When an employer trusts an employee, the employer may ask something special such as closing up the business at the end of the day.

position of trust. When an employer trusts an employee, it often means that the employer can ask the employee to do something above and beyond the call of duty and expect the employee to accomplish it. The special task could be closing up the business at the end of the day. It might involve taking the company car to another city to pick up a business associate. Each of these situations requires that the employer trust the employee to carry out the task. When the employee completes the task, he or she earns the employer's or supervisor's trust. This trust contributes to good human relations between employers and employees.

Honesty

Another trait closely allied to trust is honesty. This is a trait that gets a lot of attention in many organizations. Establishing a reputation for honesty is important in developing a good relationship with an employer, especially because one of the greatest problems in organizations is dishonest employees.

To be an honest employee means several things. It means, of course, never to take any money or goods that don't belong to you. It means never to say you worked longer than you actually did. It means never to cheat or dishonor a customer, another employee, or your employer in any way. It can also mean telling your employer and others the truth when you are questioned. If you prove to be an honest employee, you will be well on your way to acceptability and good human relations in any organization.

Responsibleness

A responsible employee is one who carries out the assigned tasks and duties as expected by the employer. Employees are often put in positions where they are responsible for money, for other people's safety, for other people's production, for merchandise, for customers' goodwill, for company equipment, and so on. Employers are quick to see which employees can handle positions and situations of responsibility and which cannot. Needless to say, employers like to have employees who are responsible persons.

Usually employers begin by asking employees to be responsible for less important things. Then they gradually make employees responsible for more important matters. This gradual buildup of responsibility leads to rewards and good relationships between employers and employees.

Let us look at the case of Valery, a new employee of Pete's Flower Shop. Soon after she was hired, Valery was asked to drive the store van to the airport to pick up a small shipment of flowers from Hawaii and to keep them cool. She made it to the airport all right. But on the way back to the store, Valery stopped by a friend's house, turned off the van's engine, and talked awhile. While the engine was stopped, the van's air conditioner was not keeping the flowers cool. They were all ruined from the heat. In this case, Valery did not prove herself to be a responsible employee. Her employer would naturally hesitate to give her a task that involves greater responsibility in the future.

Industriousness

Industrious employees work hard. This does not necessarily mean physically tiring labor. Rather, industrious means being diligent about one's duties at work. It is doing what one is paid to do, and possibly more. An industrious person does not loaf, daydream, or otherwise spend large amounts of nonproductive time. Industrious employees try to accomplish their assigned work within the prescribed time. They keep themselves productively occupied during work hours. Industrious employees will volunteer on their own, do things without being asked or assigned, and will ask for additional assignments when necessary.

It has been said that hard work is its own reward. That is, the satisfied feeling one gets when a good day's work is finished or when a task is completed is a rewarding experience. Furthermore, hard work by an employee is soon rewarded by an employer. Employers are quick to note which of their employees are hardworking and productive and which are "goofing off." The industrious workers are usually rewarded with better pay, promotions, and special privileges.

In summary, when a company hires a person, it expects that person to contribute to the success and growth of the company. Employees can contribute to their employer's success and growth by developing competence, loyalty, trustworthiness, honesty, responsibleness, and industriousness. An employee who possesses these desirable traits will enjoy a very good working relationship with any employer.

Illustration 4-8
Valery was not acting responsibly; all the flowers in the van were wilted.

CHECK YOUR UNDERSTANDING

To be sure you are reading and learning the key points, fill in the blanks with the missing word or group of words.

1. Organizational effectiveness depends on the degree to which you understand _____.

2. In developing a good relationship with an employer, it helps to remember that every _____.

3. List three ways an employer may be successful.

4. What are the main sections of the employee's part of an unwritten employment contract?

5. What do employers expect from empoyees?

EMPLOYERS MAY BE COACHES AND MENTORS

Your career may be enhanced if your employer becomes your coach and even more so if your employer is your mentor. When your employer or manager serves as your coach, it is like having a private tutor. Coaches help you learn the inner workings of the organization by:

- Providing advice and giving you the benefit of her or his experience.
- Assisting you in making contacts that will help you in your work.
- Directing you to sources of useful information.
- Serving as a sounding board for your ideas and then helping you try out those ideas on others.
- Giving you feedback on your work performance and your interpersonal behavior.

You have the responsibility for establishing the coaching relationship. To do this, you must demonstrate that you are coachable and worth the investment of your employer. The best way to show you are coachable is to develop the traits described earlier in this chapter. You must also initiate coaching sessions with your employer. During these sessions ask for help, advice, information, or feedback. Let your employer know you want his or her guidance. If you sincerely ask for your employer's counsel, you will help develop your employer into your coach.

A mentor is a special coach who takes a personal interest in your career development. Coaches become mentors for at least three reasons. The first reason is that you have demonstrated that your work is better than the work of others in your group or unit. At the same time, you have been able to balance the need for teamwork with your individual success. A second reason is that employers or managers have a duty to find and develop talent and future leaders. A third reason your employer or manager may mentor you is that she or he likes and respects you.

Unfortunately, you may have little control over whether someone likes you. You do have a great deal of control over being disliked! When employers like you enough to be your mentor, it may be because you remind them of themselves or of someone in the past who they liked or admired.

The care and development that your mentor gives may include

- ◆ Assuring that you have growth opportunities such as working on special projects, task forces, or committees.
- ◆ Giving you exposure or visibility to key people in the organization.
- ◆ Coaching you on your work and behavior (as described in the section on coaching).
- ◆ Sponsoring you for promotions to greater responsibility (and, perhaps, greater pay).
- ◆ Promoting you when the mentor is promoted.

Your responsibilities in establishing a mentoring relationship with an employer or manager are (1) demonstrating you are coachable, (2) showing appreciation for the special opportunities you receive, and (3) working smarter and harder to prove you are worthy of the mentoring efforts of your manager or employer.

BASIC MANAGEMENT STYLES OF EMPLOYERS

One of an employer's main jobs is to manage people. Managing people means keeping track of and directing the work of employees. Managing people may include determining work hours and planning work schedules. It could include solving problems and giving praise where it is due. Managing people often involves hiring and terminating employees.

There are different ways in which the job of managing employees is carried out. These ways are called management styles. An employee who wishes to be effective in the organization should try to identify the employer's management style. Once an employee does this, he or she is well on the way to good relations with the employer and a high degree of organizational effectiveness.

There are many management styles and they are slightly different from one another. They also differ in popularity among employees. However, management styles can usually be classified into three basic categories: (1) authoritarian, (2) democratic, and (3) laissez-faire

Illustration 4-9
Let your employer know you want his or her guidance.

(pronounced "lay say fair"). Each of these basic management styles has its identifying characteristics. See if you can identify any characteristics that will help you recognize the management style of the three different managers described in the following paragraphs.

AUTHORITARIAN MANAGEMENT STYLE

Mr. Brandigan is the owner and manager of a service station. He has owned and managed the station for many years. He takes a great deal of pride in referring to the station as "his" business. He started his business all by himself with very little money and a lot of hard work. His business has now increased in size so that he must employ several persons.

Each of Mr. Brandigan's employees reports directly to him. He tells them what hours to work, what clothing to wear, and when they should take their breaks. He instructs them to come to him with all of their questions. Rarely does he ask advice from any of his employees. Mr. Brandigan likes to be in charge of the entire business. His relationship with his employees is definitely that of a leader with a group of followers.

Mr. Brandigan displays the characteristics of an authoritarian leader. This style of leadership, or management style, allows employees little freedom to think, plan, and make decisions on their own. Some people react negatively to this style, while others like it. Some employees feel that it is easier to work for an authoritarian employer because they want to avoid, whenever possible, the difficult tasks of planning and decision making. Those employees who need a great deal of direction in order to be effective would most likely get along very well with an authoritarian employer.

Illustration 4-11
Many employees appreciate an opportunity to become involved in the democratic management of a company.

Illustration 4-10
Mr. Brandigan runs his business with an authoritarian style of management.

DEMOCRATIC MANAGEMENT STYLE

Ms. Fernandez owns a company that also employs several people. She holds many meetings during which she seeks the advice and ideas of her employees. For example, Ms. Fernandez encourages her employees to help her determine their vacation schedules, sick-leave policies, and parking lot arrangements. She is often gone from the office, leaving others in charge. In general, she encourages them to work together to help her run the company.

Ms. Fernandez is a democratic leader. An employer who uses the democratic leadership

> *Success isn't permanent,
> and failure isn't fatal.*
>
> - Mike Ditka

style allows employees to participate in the management of the company by seeking their ideas and suggestions. As a result, this is also known as the participative management style. It is designed to profit from the ideas of several people. Many employees like this management style because it allows them to feel as though they are really a part of the company. It makes them think that their ideas are worth something. Others dislike this style because they feel that it is clumsy and inefficient. Such employees feel that decision making is the boss's job and that they are there just to work.

LAISSEZ-FAIRE MANAGEMENT STYLE

Beth and Julius Bergman are licensed interior designers. They own and operate a business that specializes in the interior design of large city apartments. The Bergmans have hired two professional designers to work for them. They assign customers to each of these professional employees and then leave the employees on their own. That is, these professional employees are free to decide how much time to spend with each customer, how many hours they wish to work, which is the best way to work with each customer, and even how much money to charge each customer for services rendered. These professional employees were hired by the Bergmans to do a job. That job is to provide satisfactory interior decorating services. When and how these services are provided is left to the creative imagination and business experience of each employee—each to his or her own style.

As you can see, the Bergmans are laissez-faire leaders. Laissez-faire literally means "hands off," and this is the way the Bergmans deal with their employees. Note that the main characteristic of the laissez-faire style of management is employee freedom. Many employees are comfortable with this management style, but some are not. There are employees who become frustrated when faced with this much freedom because they have always had directions given to them and plans made for them. Such employees are afraid that their employer might not like what they create.

To summarize, each of these basic management styles has aspects that some people like and others dislike. Although at times an employer may use a mixture of styles, it is important to realize that most employers have management styles that can be readily identi-

Illustration 4-12
When delegating duties, the employer may make one employee responsible for managing his or her own activities and those of others.

fied. It is important because, once these styles are understood, the employee who wishes to develop a good relationship with an employer will be able to deal more effectively with the particular management style of that employer. An employee should develop such skills as independence, flexibility, and responsiveness to be able to adapt to different management styles. A good relationship will result when employee skills and management styles are matched.

QUALITY AND ORGANIZATIONAL EFFECTIVENESS

All managers, regardless of their management styles, strive for high quality in their organizations. They want quality people working for the organization. They want to produce quality products and deliver quality services. The United States government recognizes the importance of quality by giving an annual award. The award is called the Malcolm Baldrige National Quality Award. It is given to organizations that meet only the highest standards. A quality organization practices specific quality management principles. Some of the key principles are: follow quality processes, fix processes, not people, use facts and data to make decisions, and practice continuous improvement.

FOLLOW QUALITY PROCESSES

Most organizations have clear and easy-to-understand processes. These processes often describe what work is performed and how it is to be performed. Processes, for example, describe how to assemble an automobile, inspect computer chips, or make pizza. The main processes used by most pizza businesses are shown in Illustration 4-13.

Within the overall process are four main processes, and within each of these there are sub-processes. For example, the Take Customer's Order process can be broken down into the following subprocesses for a telephone order:

1. Answer the telephone and greet customer.
2. Key in customer name, address and telephone number on computer terminal.
3. Key in pizza order on computer terminal.
4. Ask if customer would like salad.
5. Ask what customer would like to drink.
6. Ask what else the customer would like.
7. Repeat the order and state the total price.
8. State cash payment policy.
9. Thank the customer for the order.
10. Verify the order was received by the pizza preparation team.

The other processes have similar subprocesses. Note that the entire process begins and ends with the customer. All quality processes begin with a customer request or customer requirement—and end when the customer requirement is met.

FIX PROCESSES NOT PEOPLE

When a customer requirement is not met, quality organizations look for problems within processes. They do not blame an individual employee. For example, if a customer did not receive the correct pizza order, the four processes would be examined to determine where the

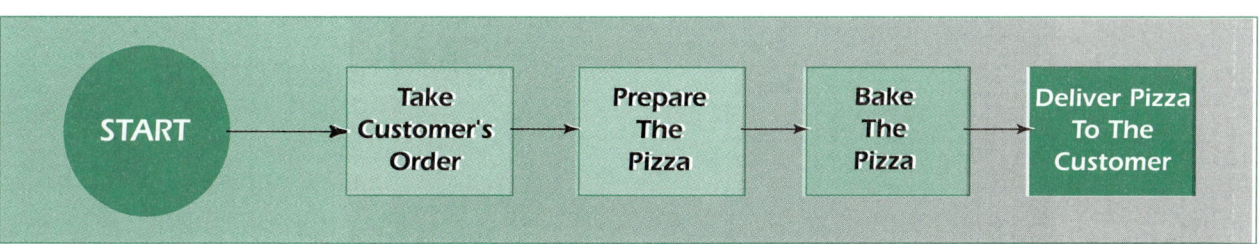

START → Take Customer's Order → Prepare The Pizza → Bake The Pizza → Deliver Pizza To The Customer

Illustration 4-13
Pizza Business Process

system broke down. It is possible that the order was taken wrong or the pizza order was prepared wrong, or it was placed in the wrong box, and so on.

This quality principle centers on the assumption that people want and try to do jobs correctly. When an error occurs we assume the process did not work or is flawed in some way. If the employee did not follow the process, then that is a performance problem and the individual is held accountable. Unfortunately, many organizations do not have well-defined processes. It is difficult, if not impossible, to fix a problem if a process is not clear to employees or if there is more than one process for the same work.

To illustrate this idea, consider the following situation. A pizza was partially burned while cooking. The manager, in dealing with the situation, says one of two things:

a. You seem to have a problem cooking pizzas. What's wrong with you?
b. Our baking process seems to have broken down. The pizza burned. What happened?

How do think an employee would feel about and react to each of these statements? Write your answers in the spaces below.

For statement (a):
_____
_____
_____
_____

For statement (b):
_____
_____
_____
_____
_____

What is the difference between the two statements?
_____
_____
_____
_____
_____
_____
_____
_____
_____

USE FACTS AND DATA TO MAKE DECISIONS

This quality principle helps people make good decisions. Decisions that are made without facts and data are not really decisions—they are guesses and opinions. For example, let's say our pizza was delivered outside of the 30-minute delivery goal in 10 of 125 deliveries. We start with a fact and some data. Note, this is not a feeling or some vague statement that "a lot of customers are complaining." The fact is that pizzas were delivered later than 30 minutes; the data tell us 10 of 125 deliveries were late. With facts and data we know if a problem exists and the size of the problem. In this example, 10 of 125 is a big problem. The question is, Why the late deliveries? The problem solving begins with a review of the processes and the collection of additional facts and data.

PRACTICE CONTINUOUS IMPROVEMENT

This quality principle is based on the belief that any process can be improved. The improvement may be faster production, shorter response time, or fewer steps in the subprocess. Improvement possibilities are unlimited. Continuous improvement applies to people, too. Here, the idea is that each person can take actions to improve his or her abilities. That, by the way, is the principle behind this book. Through study and effort we can all improve ourselves.

Can you think of some ways your school could make continuous improvement (a) in the school cafeteria or (b) in making sporting events more customer oriented? Write your answers in the spaces below.

(a) _____
_____
_____
_____
_____
_____

(b) _____
_____
_____
_____
_____
_____

WHAT IT'S LIKE TO BE AN EMPLOYER

In your study of human relations, there are two reasons why it will be helpful for you to assume the role of an employer. First, it will help you understand human relations and management from an employer's point of view. Second, because someday you may be an employer or manager yourself.

Pretend for a moment that you are the owner of a business. As the owner or manager you are responsible for many things. You must see to it that the company maintains a reputation for

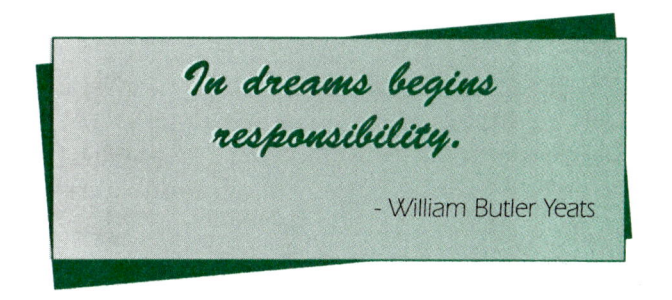

> *In dreams begins responsibility.*
>
> - William Butler Yeats

honesty and quality. The company must not only promptly pay all of its debts, but also earn a profit. It needs to remain on good terms with its suppliers. It also needs to remain on good terms with other firms in the community. Accurate financial records must be kept by the company. Also, the company premises must be kept neat and clean, as well as safe, both for customers and employees. These are only some of your many responsibilities.

As an employer, during a typical day at work you will be the first to arrive, the last to leave, and sometimes both. You will spend a lot of time talking on the telephone and meeting with employees and customers. You will have very little time for yourself. You will also have little time to think over decisions. Most of your decisions will deal with who does what, how much time is given to get something done, and how much money will be spent on equipment or supplies. At any moment you will be expected to referee disagreements between employees or with customers. You must show personal interest in each employee, but stop short of getting involved in personal lives.

The ultimate responsibility for successfully running an organization rests with its owner or manager. This person must ensure that everything and everybody in the organization works, and works together. To carry responsibility for all the duties involved in running an organization is usually too much for one person alone. This is why a delegation of duties takes place. This means that the employer or manager assigns certain responsibilities and duties to various employees. The larger the organization, the more duties are delegated.

For example, the employer may make one employee responsible for keeping the financial records. Another employee may be assigned to keep the premises clean. Still another might be made responsible for maintaining good relationships with other firms in the community. But the responsibility for getting along with one another lies with each and every employee.

An employer, therefore, is most pleased when all the employees carry out the responsibilities given them. Now that you have a fairly good idea of what it's like to be an employer, you should try your best to carry out all responsibilities given to you and work hard to maintain good relations with your employer.

CHECK YOUR UNDERSTANDING

To be sure you are reading and learning the key points, fill in the blanks with the missing word or group of words.

1. Coaches help you understand the inner workings of the organization by (list two ways).
_____
_____

2. Your responsibilities in establishing a mentoring relationship with an employer are
_____
_____
_____ .

3. This style of management allows employees little freedom to plan and make decisions on their own. It is
_____

4. The participative management style is known as
_____ .

5. Four principles of quality management are:
_____
_____
_____
_____

6. What are characteristics of a typical day in the work life of an employer?
_____
_____
_____
_____
_____

NET WORKING

Join us on the Internet. Check out our Human Relations for Career Success Home Page.

Try some of our special Internet Activities on organizational effectiveness for Chapter 4. Your instructor will give you instructions on which activities would be good for you to complete.

Connect with us at:

http://success.swpco.com

Activity 4-1
INTERVIEWING AN EMPLOYER

Yes, employers are human. This activity will provide an opportunity for you to find out firsthand. Arrange to interview two employers in your community. Select two different types of employers: from a large business and a small business; from a retail and a wholesale business; from a profit and a nonprofit organization; from a service business and a product business.

The interviews will help you get to know an employer and will get you started toward good relations with employers. To help you with the interviews, a list of questions you might ask is given on the next page. In the spaces provided, jot down the answers given to you during the interviews.

When the interviews are complete, compare the answers of the two different employers:

1. What answers are the same or nearly the same?

2. What answers are different?

3. What unexpected answers did you receive?

EMPLOYER QUESTIONNAIRE

1. How long have you been an employer?

2. What is the purpose of your organization (why does it exist)?

3. What are your goals for this year?

4. Do you like your job? Why?

5. Does your work sometimes make you irritable or upset? When does this happen?

6. Who are your competitors? Do you worry about your competitors getting your customers' business?

7. Do you have a mentor? Are you mentoring someone? Why or why not? (Note: Be ready to explain what you mean by mentoring.)

8. What is the best part of your job? Why is it the best part?

Activity 4-2
YOUR MISSION IS . . .

Every organization has a reason for existing. And, everyone who works has a reason for working. If you are employed, complete Part I of this activity. If you are not employed, complete Part II of this activity.

Part I - FOR EMPLOYED STUDENTS

Read each question carefully. Then write your answers in the spaces provided.

1. What is the purpose of the organization for which you work? Why does it exist? To obtain this information, ask your employer or supervisor. Be prepared to share your information with the class.

   _____
   _____
   _____
   _____
   _____
   _____

2. Why are you working for this organization? To help answer this question, refer to the Employer and Employee Expectations part of this chapter.

   _____
   _____
   _____
   _____
   _____
   _____

3. Do your reasons for working have anything in common with the reason the organization exists? Can you adjust your reasons for working so that they support the purpose of the organization?

   _____
   _____
   _____
   _____
   _____
   _____

Part II - FOR STUDENTS WHO ARE NOT EMPLOYED

Read each question carefully. Then write your answers in the spaces provided.

1. In Activity 4-1, you asked an employer about the purpose of his or her organization. Rewrite that answer below.

2. If you were working at the organization in Question 1 above, why would you work for this organization? To help answer this question, refer to the Employer and Employee Expectations part of this chapter.

3. Do your reasons for working have anything in common with the reason the organization exists? Can you adjust your reasons for working so that they support the purpose of the organization?

Activity 4-3
LIFE IS NOT FAIR

Read the following case study. Then think about the questions that follow. Answer the questions in the space provided.

Case Study

Rochelle and Mike are new employees at the Rock Café. They work the front counter selling Rock Café trademarked items such as T-shirts, key chains, bumper stickers, jewelry, mugs, and the like. During the second week at work, Mike noticed that his work hours were less than Rochelle's. Over several weeks, Rochelle was scheduled to work more frequently than Mike.

Mike liked his work and he quickly learned to process credit card purchases and place out-of-stock orders on the inventory system. When he and Rochelle worked together, Mike had to help her with almost all of the credit card purchases. It seemed to Mike that Rochelle spent most of the time talking to the manager and other employees rather than helping customers.

As time goes by, Mike is becoming more and more unhappy working at the Rock Café.

---

1. Do you think Mike's unwritten employment contract has been broken by the Rock Café? If so, what part of the contract?

Activity 4-3, continued

2. What is Mike doing to meet his employer's unwritten expectations?

3. Do some people seem to get better treatment than others? Why?

4. What should Mike do about his situation?

5. What parts of your unwritten employment contract are (will be) most important to you?

Activity 4-4
DEALING WITH AUTHORITARIAN, DEMOCRATIC, AND LAISSEZ-FAIRE EMPLOYERS

You have read about three leadership or management styles an employer may adopt. After reading the situations given below in Illustration 4-14, write in the blank spaces how you think an employer with each style would react to each situation.

Situation	Authoritarian	Democratic	Laissez-Faire
You are a salesperson and an irate customer continues to harass you weekly about the low quality of the goods the store sells.			
You are a hospital admissions clerk and a person comes to your desk wishing to solicit contributions for a charity from the nurses and physicians.			
You and one other employee want a cold-drink machine installed in the employees' lounge.			

Illustration 4-14
Different management styles.

Activity 4-5
WHAT LEADERSHIP STYLE WOULD YOU CHOOSE?

Assume that you are the owner of a small convenience food store. At the bottom of this page, and on the next page if you need it, tell which management style you would adopt (Authoritarian, democratic, or laissez-faire) and why you would adopt that particular style. Then discuss your answers in class.

Activity 4-5, continued

Activity 4-6
QUALITY MANAGEMENT

This activity will help you understand quality management principles. We have used the pizza business to describe four principles of quality:

1. Following quality processes
2. Fixing processes, not people
3. Using facts and data to make decisions
4. Practicing continuous improvement

Divide into small groups of three to five people.

Select two or more pizza businesses in your area. If national organizations such as Pizza Hut and Domino's are in your area, include them in your selection. National organizations often have very specific ways of doing business that are consistent from store to store.

Make an appointment with the restaurant manager to discuss the pizza business processes.

Visit the business and discuss the quality principles you have learned in this chapter. Ask about:

- process documentation and process training
- process measurements, particularly time requirements
- problems and how facts and data help in solving the problems
- examples of continuous improvement

Present what you learned to the class.

5 INTERPERSONAL COMMUNICATION

KNOWLEDGE

After reading this chapter, you will be able to:

✓ Define **communication** and draw a model of the communication process.
✓ Analyze the statement, "Meanings are in people, not in words."
✓ Describe and give examples of the problem of semantics.
✓ Define **allness** and apply the definition to daily communications.
✓ Apply the following principles of listening to situations in the business world:
   a. People think faster than they speak.
   b. Emotions block out certain messages.
   c. Planning a reply gets in the way of listening.
✓ Explain the meaning of "Listen for facts and feelings."
✓ List three or more ways to improve listening.
✓ Draw formal and informal communication systems, using principles of the formal organization chart.
✓ Describe the relationship of the rumor formula to accuracy of the grapevine.
✓ Apply principles of business etiquette to electronic communications.

ATTITUDES

After reading this chapter, you will:

✓ Believe that meanings are in people, not in words.
✓ Recognize the damage to human relations caused by allness.
✓ Be concerned about the negative aspects of labeling and emotionally loaded words, as well as sexist language.
✓ Appreciate listening for facts and feelings in a message.
✓ Gain satisfaction from improved listening.
✓ Accept the limitations of the grapevine communication system.
✓ Value the use of formal communication in organizations.

This year employers will spend millions of dollars trying to improve communication in their organizations. Similar amounts were invested last year, and even more money will be spent next year. Employers will spend thousands of hours attending communication-training programs, and thousands of hours will be devoted to communication training for employees. By spending so much time and money on improving communication, one would think that communication problems were under control. The opposite is true. Communication problems are far from being under control.

All of this time and money, however, has not been wasted. Many organizations now have colorful company magazines, exciting web sites, eye-catching newsletters, and well-written office memos. Some companies even send birthday cards to their employees. Unfortunately, these kinds of efforts have little effect on improving communication. Why? Because the main problems center on the failure of people to recognize that communication problems are human problems. Emotions, attitudes, and feelings are involved whenever people communicate. The barriers to good communication are a result of human problems.

DEFINITION OF COMMUNICATION

Most managers cannot define good communication. In a recent survey, managers were asked, "What is good communication?" They gave answers such as:

1. Good communication . . . is when workers have good attitudes.
2. Good communication . . . happens when employee turnover is low.
3. Good communication . . . eliminates misunderstandings.

As you can see, the managers responded by describing the *results* of good communication. They were not able to tell what it is, even though they knew when good communication occurred. How, then, can managers improve something they cannot define? The answer would seem to be this: only with a lot of luck. As a wise student of good human relations and communication in business, you would not wish to depend on plain luck, would you?

Communication is a process. The process, shown in Illustration 5-1, is a series of four operations. Here is how it works:

1. A person called the *Sender* wants to say something. That something is called a message.
2. The Sender then decides how the message will be sent. In most communication models, this is referred to as *channel selection*.

Examples of channels include the following:

ORAL
- face-to-face
- small group meeting
- large group meeting

WRITTEN
- notes and letters
- memos and reports

SIGN LANGUAGE

BODY LANGUAGE

TECHNOLOGY
- electronic mail
- voice mail
- fax
- telephone, pager
- videotape
- compact disk

MASS MEDIA
- radio
- television
- newspaper
- magazine
- newsletter

SPECIAL SIGNALS
- Morse code
- flashing lights
- signaling flags
- smoke signals
- drums

3. A person called the *Receiver* listens to the message and decides on a response. The response is called a *feedback*.

4. The Receiver then chooses how the feedback will be sent. Again, there is channel selection for the feedback.

All two-way communication follows the process shown in Illustration 5-1. If the communication is one way, the feedback parts of the process are not used. The process itself

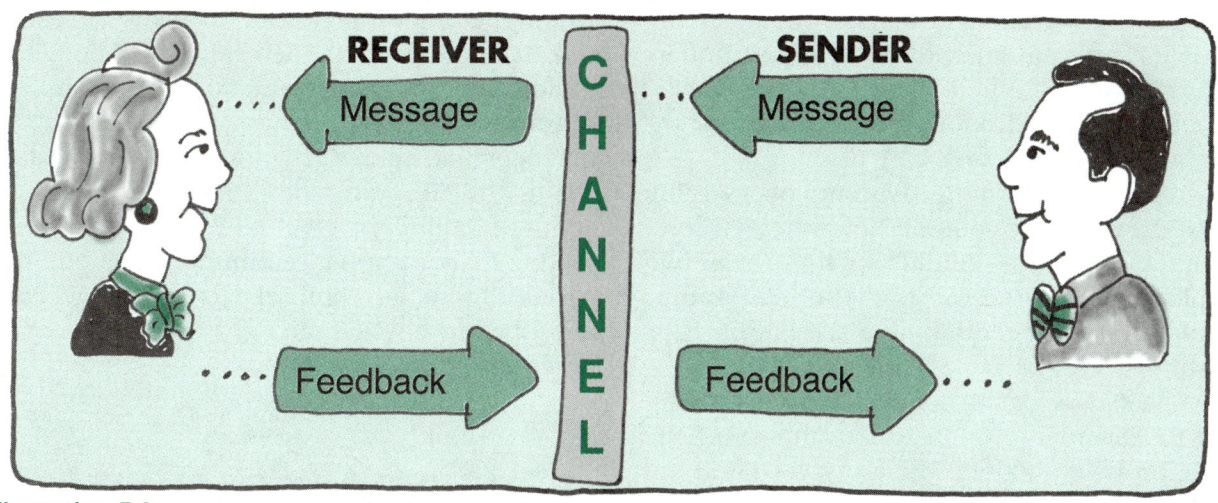

Illustration 5-1
The Communication Process

always works. Problems develop because people, knowingly or unknowingly, present barriers to the message and the feedback reception.

BARRIERS TO GOOD COMMUNICATION AND HUMAN RELATIONS

Do you think that words, by themselves, mean the same thing to everyone? If you do, you are like most people who have not studied communication problems. To illustrate this point, answer the following question:

What is the definition of the word *lead*?

The word *lead*, for example, has more than 80 different meanings! What is more, the 500 most common words in the English language have more than 14,000 different meanings. Now you can see why meanings are in people, not in words. Only people can give meaning to words. When a person uses a word, that word is used with just one definition even though the word may have several definitions. Many people overlook this simple principle of communication: Meanings are in people, not in words.

THE PROBLEM OF SEMANTICS

Semantic problems occur when people forget that a single word or expression may have different meanings. The semantic problems are further complicated by the fact that several different words may have the same meaning. For example, surely you can think of different words that mean the same as the three words listed below.

Money = _____
_____

Home = _____
_____

Car = _____
_____

Every day, somewhere conflict develops because of misunderstandings over the meanings of words. A manager may tell an employee to do something that the employee seems to understand. Yet the employee may actually end up doing the wrong thing because what he or she does is not what the manager intended to have done. Thus, a communication breakdown occurs that may cause serious human relations problems.

Ralph's mistake is an example of the problem of semantics. On Monday morning, Ralph's manager called him into the office and said, "Ralph, last week's sales were terrible! In fact, sales for the entire month are 20 percent below last year at this time. The employees seem to spend more time arguing with one another than selling. I want you to find out what the trouble is and put an end to it. Do you understand?"

"OK, boss," replied Ralph, who was the manager's assistant. "I'll take care of it."

On Tuesday morning, two employees came up to the manager's office. They were extremely upset! Ralph had found out that these two employees were the cause of the many arguments that had been taking place. So he fired them!

Ralph's boss could not believe what Ralph did. He meant for Ralph to straighten out the situation when he said, "I want you to find out what the trouble is and put an end to it." To Ralph, the solution meant something entirely different. The manager forgot that meanings are in people, not in words.

Communication problems that result from problems of semantics can be avoided if the manager practices two important rules of communication. First, a manager must recognize that words by themselves have different meanings. Second, the manager must ask employees what they understood, not if they understood. Too many problems begin when a manager asks, "Do you understand?" or "Do you have any questions?" This question is not a good form of communication because any employee would be under pressure to answer, "Yes, I understand," even though he or she does not understand. In the case of Ralph, the communication problem could have been avoided if the manager had said, "Tell me what you understand," or "Tell me what you are going to do about it, Ralph." Surely it takes an extra minute to think about good communication, but the cost is small when compared to the cost of problems that arise when the right questions are not asked.

THE PROBLEM OF ALLNESS

A manager or employee who believes that what she or he says is absolute, complete, certain, or final is guilty of allness. The tone of allness is suggested by the use of such words as always, ever, and never. This problem of allness is more common than one might think. It is illustrated in conversations that take place every day.

Oversimplification

The problem of allness often occurs because of the tendency to simplify things. A person makes things simple by reducing something

Illustration 5-2
The tone of allness is suggested by the use of the word *always*.

large to something small. When something is small, it is easier to remember. To illustrate the process of oversimplification, let us take the example of a motorist who stops to ask a service station attendant for directions to a certain place.

Motorist: How do I get to Mile High Stadium?

Attendant: Well, go down this street you're on for three blocks. Turn right at the four-way stop, then go to the second stoplight and turn left. It will be about a half mile on your right—you can't miss it.

Motorist: Let's see now, right at the four-way, two stop lights and a left, half mile on my right.

In this example, the motorist repeats the directions given by simplifying the main parts. The motorist does not repeat the full statement of directions.

The Sample-of-One Judgment

When it comes to any business or employment conditions, however, over-simplification can result in an especially dangerous problem of allness. It can have a bad effect on human relations.

For example, Mrs. Marvin, the chief supervisor of a hospital, likes to talk with the employees from time to time. She walks through the food service area and talks to one employee. Then she walks around the second floor and talks with a nurse. Mrs. Marvin talks to another nurse on the third floor and does the same thing on the fourth and fifth floors. Finally she goes back to her office and thinks about the things that were said to her. She remembers the food service worker complaining about the part-time employees who were not taking work seriously. Mrs. Marvin also remembers that the nurse on the second floor complained about the janitors who were not cleaning the floors properly. Each of the nurses on the third, fourth, and fifth floors talked in very general terms, not saying much of anything.

Mrs. Marvin then concludes that things are going well on the third, fourth, and fifth floors. She also concludes that there are problems on the second floor and in food service. Therefore, at a later conference with the head of food service, Mrs. Marvin made the following remark:

"I hear the part-time workers are not doing good work." The head of food service did not know what to say because Mrs. Marvin's statement was not absolutely true. Mrs. Marvin had talked with only one person, yet she made a judgment about the part-time workers. This was a sample-of-one judgment—a judgment based on a statement from only one person. Mrs. Marvin was not aware that she was making the judgment based on such little evidence. Her case is a classic example of the problem of allness—making a dangerous sample-of-one judgment without knowing what she was doing.

EitherOr Thinking

Oversimplification often leads to EitherOr ("either . . or . . . ") thinking. EitherOr thinking presents situations as having only two choices or outcomes. For example, Tim was upset about a situation at work. His thinking was, "Either she apologizes, or I'll quit." After thinking about the situation, Tim decided quitting was not in his best interest. He then concluded, "If she does not apologize, I'll report her for being late." Twice, Tim's thinking was limited to two EitherOr alternatives.

Another characteristic of EitherOr thinking is the tendency for at least one of the alternatives to be extreme. For example the statement, "If you can't report on time, then don't bother showing up" contains an extreme alternative. Following are a few Either statements. Add the Or part of the statement. Try to make the Or an extreme alternative. Compare your answers with others in class.

EITHER . . .	OR . . .
Buy the red one . . .	_____
	_____
Tell me exactly what happened . . .	_____
	_____
Answer the phone on one ring . . .	_____
	_____

Although EitherOr thinking appears to make sense, it does not match reality. In the real world, there are rarely only two choices. Think of the EitherOr outcomes first on a scale of 1 to 3 and then on a scale of 1 to 10.

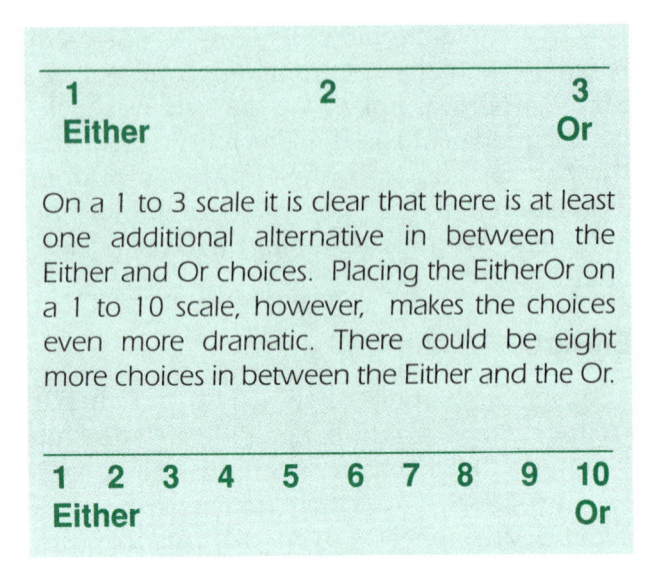

1	2	3
Either		Or

On a 1 to 3 scale it is clear that there is at least one additional alternative in between the Either and Or choices. Placing the EitherOr on a 1 to 10 scale, however, makes the choices even more dramatic. There could be eight more choices in between the Either and the Or.

1	2	3	4	5	6	7	8	9	10
Either									Or

Another way to deal with EitherOr is to think "It's not *either or*; it may be *both or neither*." For example, "Do you want onion or green pepper on your pizza?" Some people would prefer both; others do not like either green pepper or onion on pizza. Here is one last thought on EitherOr thinking. When problem solving and decision making it's OK to start with two choices. The challenge is to get past this limited two-choice thinking and move to higher-quality thinking with many choices.

MISUSE OF LANGUAGE

Employers and employees can cause communication problems by misusing language. Two of the most serious communication problems that arise because of the misuse of language are (1) labeling, or name calling, and (2) emotional confusion.

Labeling, or Name Calling

Name calling, or *labeling*, means to unfairly classify someone as a certain type of person.

Typical labels given to people are:

1. Clown—a person who appears to do silly things on a regular basis.
2. Troublemaker—a person who appears to be frequently involved in controversy.
3. Animal—a person lacking in manners.

Labeling is a twofold human relations problem. That is, two things can happen when a person has been labeled: (1) the person will tend to *live up* to the label, or (2) the person will do dangerous things to *live down* the label.

Living Up to a Label. Here is an example of a person who lives up to a label. Ben, a sales management trainee, worked in a large office with about a hundred co-workers. On his first day in the office, Ben noticed that some old screwdrivers and small pliers were left in the desk he inherited. That very afternoon the tools came in handy. An employee's laptop computer would not close properly and Ben was able to fix it.

Ben enjoyed being helpful. He soon earned the reputation of "Mr. Fixit." As time went by, Ben began volunteering to fix loose computer cables, add memory chips, and help with software questions. Attempting to fix a telephone, however, proved to be Ben's downfall. After working on the telephone for a half hour, Ben accidentally dropped it on his toe. The telephone broke into a few large pieces and numerous small pieces.

The results of Ben's sincere effort to be helpful were surprising. Ben's co-worker, who

Illustration 5-3
Labeling means to unfairly classify someone as a certain type of person.

Illustration 5-4
Jill tried to live down her label of "Miss Fashion."

relied on the telephone for a large volume of productivity, was unproductive for a day while waiting for a replacement phone. Ben had to be sent to the company medical department to have his toe checked. This resulted in several hours of lost productivity to Ben and some unnecessary medical paperwork for Ben's supervisor. Moreover, the company union was upset because Ben was doing "craft" work. This resulted in more lost hours of productivity because the union requested to meet with Ben's supervisor to discuss this small, but, to them, significant breach of the labor contract. Ben's efforts to live up to his label turned out to be expensive!

Living Down a Label. This example tells about a person who tries to live down a label. Jill's first week at her new job was unpleasant. She wanted to look nice, so she dressed up. Jill had her hair styled and really looked good. The trouble was, she looked *too good*. No one said much to her that first week. On Friday, some of her co-workers let her know that she was overdressed.

Although Jill got the message about being overdressed, it was too late. Her co-workers had begun to unkindly refer to her as "Miss Fashion." During her second week at work, Jill dressed like everyone else did. But the nickname Miss Fashion stuck, and Jill didn't like it. She therefore began to dress down by wearing sloppy clothes. That didn't work, and the nickname stayed with her. Jill continued to dress even more sloppily. Finally, Jill's supervisor had to talk to her about her careless, slovenly appearance. In her efforts to live down her label, Jill suffered some problems. She became upset with her co-workers, and her supervisor became upset with her.

Emotional Confusion

Earlier in this chapter you learned that a word can have many different meanings. You also learned that several words can mean the same thing.

Use Pleasant-Sounding Words or Titles. Among words that mean the same thing, some have a pleasant association and others do not. At work, especially, it is important to emphasize the positive side of things by using words that sound pleasant. For example, who would want to buy *death insurance*? Probably very few. However, *life insurance* is being sold to millions of people.

Would you prefer to buy luggage that is labeled *imitation leather* or *leatherette*? Both are the same. Grocery stores don't sell *hamburger*—they do sell *ground beef*.

A group of words that also appeal to the emotions consists of occupational titles. For example, which of the following titles would you prefer?

Negative Appeal (–)	Positive Appeal (+)
garbage collector	sanitation worker
shrink	psychologist
cop	police officer
disk jockey	radio personality
cook	chef
driver	chauffer

The words and occupational titles are not problems in themselves. They only serve to illustrate this point: *You can say things in a positive tone, and you can say the same things in a negative tone.*

Watch Out for Emotionally Loaded Words. Emotional confusion results when people forget that some words have a negative asociation, or sound unpleasant to others. Such words are called *emotionally loaded words*. Some examples of emotionally loaded words and their positive counterparts follow:

Emotionally Loaded Words	Less Emotionally Loaded Words
cheap	inexpensive
sick	ill
fired	asked to resign
worried	concerned
lie	not true
pop quiz	unscheduled test

Although the emotionally loaded words listed above may sound all right to you, remember that to others these words may have a negative tone.

Forgetting that some words are emotionally loaded can cause a serious human relations problem. For example, one afternoon Mrs. Walton, general manager of the Central Lumber Company, walked out of her office to the cash register area. Three employees were standing by the register and talking. Mrs. Walton told the employees to stop gossiping and to straighten the counter displays. She did not think that the word *gossiping* was emotionally loaded, for she often used it. As a result, one of the employees became very upset. He was not a gossip, and he resented Mrs. Walton's use of this word. To this employee a *gossip* was a very crude and disgusting person.

Another example is Stan, an airline flight attendant, who forgot about emotionally loaded words. As the plane was flying into some stormy weather, Stan announced over the loud-speakers: "We are approaching a *storm*. Please fasten your seat belts for your own safety." This announcement disturbed the passengers of Flight 105. Stan should have said: "We are approaching some bumpy air. Please fasten your seat belts. You will be more comfortable."

Avoid Sexist Language. A common misuse of language that results in human relations problems is sexist language. Such language indicates prejudicial discrimination against both men and women, but more often against women.

For example, a male manager wrote on the performance appraisal of a female subordinate: "friendly and bubbly." The term *bubbly*, although intended to be positive, is not a term generally attributable to *both* sexes. The manager was guilty of sexist language. He would have been better off using only the adjective "friendly."

Following is a list of sexist words that at one time were thought to be acceptable. To the right of each word is an appropriate term (nonsexist) for today's standards.

Sexist	Nonsexist
foreman	supervisor
businessman	business executive
insurance man	insurance agent
chairman	chairperson
manpower	work force
mankind	humanity
Congressman	Representative
housewife	homemaker
usherette	usher
policeman	police officer
mailman	letter carrier
fireman	firefighter

> *It's a rare person who wants to hear what he or she doesn't want to hear.*
>
> - Dick Cavett

Tips on Avoiding the Misuse of Language

It is possible to avoid communication problems caused by labeling and the use of emotionally loaded words. Here are some tips to help you:

1. Don't react to labels. If someone labels you, remember that the person is expressing an opinion. Everyone has a right to his or her opinion. You need not agree with it. Remember that there are many other people in your life who do not try to label you.
2. Avoid labeling others; practice empathy. Empathy means seeing the world through the eyes of the other person. You would not like to be labeled. Don't label others.
3. Use positively loaded words to describe things. You will rarely offend someone by referring to the good side of things, people, or events.
4. Be constantly ready to explain your intentions in a non-defensive way. When someone reacts the opposite way from the way you thought the person would, stop talking and start explaining. The easiest way to do this is to say, "I didn't mean it that way; let me try again."

To summarize this section, remember that good communication will improve human relations. Sharing and understanding messages is only the beginning of good communication. Remember that meanings are in people, not in words. When you hear someone making absolute statements, be alert for communication problems. Watch out for labels and for emotionally loaded words. Good listening, which will be discussed in the next section of this chapter, will help you be aware of these things.

CHECK YOUR UNDERSTANDING

To be sure you are reading and learning the key points, fill in the blanks with the missing word or group of words.

1. What are the four elements of the communication process?
_____
_____
_____
_____

2. Give an example to show that meanings are in people, not in words.
_____
_____
_____

3. How do you detect allness?
_____
_____
_____

4. What is EitherOr thinking?
_____
_____
_____

5. Give two examples of emotionally loaded and then less emotionally loaded words.
_____
_____

6. What is sexist language and why is it inappropriate?
_____
_____
_____
_____

Illustration 5-5
A good listener thinks about what is being said.

THE IMPORTANCE OF GOOD LISTENING

Listening requires more than just hearing. A good listener thinks about what is being said. When a good listener does not understand a message, he or she asks the speaker for a different explanation. A good listener must be alert. Listening is much more than hearing. The process of listening requires an active mind.

People at work spend more time in listening than in any other form of communication. Experts in communication generally agree that, in a typical workday, people spend the following amounts of time on the different forms of communication:

Listening	45 percent of the day
Speaking	30 percent of the day
Reading	15 percent of the day
Writing	10 percent of the day

Unfortunately, most people do not truly listen to what is being said. They may hear, but they do not listen. At work it is especially important to acquire the habit of good listening because this is good communication. And good communication promotes good human relations.

WHY PEOPLE DON'T LISTEN WELL

There are three main reasons why people are poor listeners. These are: (1) people think faster than they speak, (2) emotions block out certain messages, and (3) planning a reply gets in the way of listening.

People Think Faster Than They Speak

The human brain operates at an amazingly high speed. On the average, a person's brain can process 500 or 700 words a minute. Yet most people talk at a rate of about 125 words a

Illustration 5-6
The time gap between thinking and talking may result in a listening problem.

minute. This time gap results in a listening problem. The brain finds it very easy to listen and, at the same time, to think other thoughts. When this happens, the mind begins to wander. As a result, listening is not consistent because people allow themselves to be distracted. This kind of listening is often covered up by pretending to listen when, in fact, the listener is thinking other thoughts.

Emotions Block Out Some Messages

Emotions color one's understanding of what is being said. When a person is involved in a situation, he or she is likely to listen with bias. Certain signals can serve to warn you that emotions may be interfering with your listening. These signals are (1) when you resent the opposition and (2) when your personality clashes with the other speaker's personality.

Resenting the Opposition. It is easy to listen to someone who agrees with you. However, it is more difficult to listen to someone with whom you do not agree.

For example, Earl has trouble listening to people who do not agree with him. He works at Building Supplies, a retail lumber and fixture store. Unfortunately, Earl loses a lot of customers because of his open resentment of any opposition to his ideas. For instance, when a customer wanted the B & B brand for a light switch, Earl said that the Levington brand was much better. When the customer preferred to buy the B & B brand, Earl got a little upset. As a result, the customer left the store while Earl went to the stockroom for the B & B switch. The customer did not wait for Earl to get the switch. How would you handle this situation? What would you do differently? Write your answer in the spaces below.

_____
_____
_____
_____
_____
_____
_____
_____

Clashing Personalities. It is much easier to listen to someone you like. Listening to someone you don't like can be a problem. When we don't like the speaker, we tend to do one of four things:

1. We give attention to how the speaker is saying things and what items the speaker is emphasizing. Then we question whether we like the speaker's tone or emphasis.
2. We listen for areas of disagreement instead of agreement. When we hear something we disagree with, we "turn off" the message.
3. We allow the speaker's distracting habits or mannerisms to capture our attention.
4. We look at the way the speaker is dressed and find fault.

In short, we allow the speaker's personality to block the message.

A personality clash at work can sometimes result in a costly experience. For example, Roberta did not like Ricardo, her co-worker. One Monday morning Ricardo called the office to say that he would not be at work on time. It was Roberta who answered the phone. Ricardo explained why he would be late that day and then hung up. But Roberta did not really listen. All she heard Ricardo say was that he would not be in to work. At that point Roberta said to herself, "Well, good." Then Roberta reported to the supervisor that Ricardo called to say that he wouldn't be at work.

As a result of Roberta's inaccurate report, the supervisor had to call another employee, Sheila, to come to work. Although it was Sheila's day off, she agreed to work that day. When Sheila arrived at the office, however, she found Ricardo just arriving, too. Of course, Sheila became angry, but the supervisor was even angrier! Roberta had caused a lot of trouble and expense because she did not listen carefully to Ricardo, whom she disliked.

Planning a Reply Hinders Good Listening

A true conversation between two people rarely occurs. Supposedly, when two people have a conversation, one talks and the other listens. However, most often this is not the case. Most people simply do not listen to what is being said. Actually they listen for a moment of silence that will allow them to speak.

For example, as one person begins to tell about a recent activity, the other person begins to think of one of his or her own recent experiences. When the speaker pauses—and this is that moment of silence—the other person jumps into the conversation with his or her own story. Rarely does the listener respond directly to what the speaker has just said. Instead, the listener begins to talk about what he or she was thinking.

Simply listening for the moment of silence creates a communication problem. In the following dialogue, notice how no one responds to what was first said. Each speaker tells a related story, but the attempt to get a real conversation going is frustrated!

Illustration 5-7
Do you listen or do you think about what you are going to say?

Illustration 5-8
Listen for facts and for feelings.

Rob: I saw a terrific horror film on the late show last night . . .
Mike: Oh, did you see the one a week ago Friday night about Dracula?
Lany: Hey, don't you people ever sleep? I was so tired last night. I worked until midnight and then went straight home . . .
Rob: This one last night started about midnight, a good science fiction movie. The Earth was about to explode . . .

WHAT GOOD LISTENING REQUIRES

Effective listening requires two skills. These are (1) the ability to listen for facts and (2) the ability to listen for feelings.

Ability to Listen for Facts

Listening for facts comes more naturally than listening for feelings. Most people try to understand the facts while listening and consequently are able to respond to facts. Illustration 5-9 contains some statements made by a worker. What facts can you find in the worker's message?

Facts in the Message

_____
_____
_____
_____
_____

Obviously the fact in the worker's message is

this: The heating system does not work. If a listener's answer is based on facts only, that answer would probably be as follows: "Okay, I'll tell the boss and we'll do something about the heating system."

Ability to Listen for Feelings

It is important to let a person know that you're listening for his or her feelings. When a person expresses any feelings, that person wants the listener to know about the feelings that are expressed.

Look at Illustration 5-9 again. What feelings are expressed in the worker's message?

Feelings in the Message

_____
_____
_____
_____
_____

The feelings expressed by the worker could range from anger to humor. If the worker is serious, she is probably expressing any or all of the following feelings:

1. She is angry about the heating system not working.
2. She is angry at the boss.
3. She is concerned about being cold while working.

If the listener's answer is based on both facts and feelings, that answer would probably be as follows: "The heating system doesn't work, huh? No wonder you're upset. I'll tell the boss, and we'll do something about it. I know she would not want you to work in a cold room."

When a person's expressed feelings are ignored the first time around, that person will usually make a second attempt to express feelings. The following dialogue is an example.

Employee: Where in the world is Charlie? I've got a report to do. He has the books locked in his desk. He's never around when you need him.

Manager: I'll use my key to open his desk

Illustration 5-9
What are the facts in the message?

and get the books. Then you can get your report finished.

Employee: Don't bother. We'll never find the right accounts in his messy desk. If you were more strict, he'd be here. This office is the most disorganized place I've ever seen.

In the example just given, the manager failed to listen for feelings in the employee's first outburst. The second outburst of emotion could have been prevented if the manager had responded to the facts and feelings as follows: "I don't know where Charlie is. It sounds like you're upset because he should have given you the books before he left. Would it help if I unlocked the desk with my key?"

The greatest thing about responding to facts and feelings is that it works! Try it. Remember to listen for feelings. Let the person know that you are listening to feelings that are being expressed. You will be pleased with the results.

HOW TO IMPROVE LISTENING HABITS

Good listening habits will improve human relations. By listening carefully to others, you silently tell them you care about what they have to say. Here are some tips to help you improve listening:

1. Encourage others to talk. As you encourage others to speak, you feel more

responsible for listening. You also learn from and about others when they talk.

2. Use nonverbal actions to encourage the person who is talking. Look at the person while he or she is talking; nod as you hear the meaning of what is being said; say "uh-huh" and "hmm." These actions tell the person that you are listening.

3. Take advantage of your fast-working mind. Remember people can only speak about 125 words per minute. Your mind can process five times as much in the same time period. Use the extra time to repeat and rephrase what the person is saying.

4. When your mind wanders, admit it—at least to yourself. Then ask the speaker to repeat what was said.

5. Don't interrupt. Interrupting someone can cause hard feelings. Remember you are not on a quiz show. You need not blurt out an answer before the speaker has finished.

6. Prevent emotional deafness. When you sense that you are getting angry because of the speaker's message, take positive action. Avoid negative action such as turning off the message. Use your emotions for fine-tuning. Listen for assump- and for the logic in what is being said.

7. Listen for feelings as well as for facts. Listening for facts is more natural than listening for feelings; most people can get the facts in a message. Listening for a person's feelings is difficult. By listening for feelings, you improve listening in two ways. First, you will become more aware of your own emotions. When you are aware of your own emotions, you can control them. Second, as you listen for feelings, you will have a better understanding of what the speaker really means.

OFFICIAL AND UNOFFICIAL COMMUNICATION

Most people recognize that there are two systems of communication that exist at work: (1) the formal system and (2) the informal system. Communication at work can therefore be official (formal) or unofficial (informal), depending on which type of organization is used to relay the communication.

FORMAL ORGANIZATION FOR OFFICIAL COMMUNICATION

The formal system of organization allows work to be done quickly and smoothly. This system is the official way of dividing the work among all employees. It is also a way of dividing authority and responsibility among the managers and supervisors. A formal organization is usually illustrated by means of an organization chart. Illustration 5-10 shows the organization chart of a department store.

An organization chart represents the official chain of command at work. It shows the official (1) lines of authority, (2) areas of responsibility, and (3) lines of communication.

Lines of Authority

Authority is the power or right to command or lead. It is possible to tell who has authority by looking at an organization chart from top to bottom. In Illustration 5-10, the first position of authority is held by the store manager, who is at the top. The store manager has authority over all employees. The second position of authority is shared by five people. They are the personnel manager, the advertising manager, the sales manager, the finance manager, and the maintenance manager. The merchandise buyers are in the third position of authority. Each of these buyers reports to the sales manager. Next in line are the department managers, who have less authority than the merchandise buyers. At the bottom of the chart are the salespeople. As you can see, a salesperson has no authority over anyone in the store.

Areas of Responsibility

Responsibility means that a person must answer for what happens. It means accepting blame for failure or accepting credit for success.

Generally, the more duties you have, the greater the area of responsibility you have. The areas of responsibility for all employees are also shown on an organization chart. Illustration 5-10 shows that the store manager is responsible for the entire store. The sales manager is responsible for all the employees and business transactions in the sales division. The merchandise buyers help the sales manager purchase merchandise. The merchandise buyer for clothing is responsible for both the Men's Clothing Department and the Women's Clothing Department. Each department manager is responsible for everything that takes place in the department. The assistant managers help the department managers in two ways: They help keep inventories of the clothing merchandise and help supervise the salespeople.

Illustration 5-11 on the next page shows an upside-down triangle that indicates the amount of authority and responsibility held by people in an organization. The small area at the lower tip

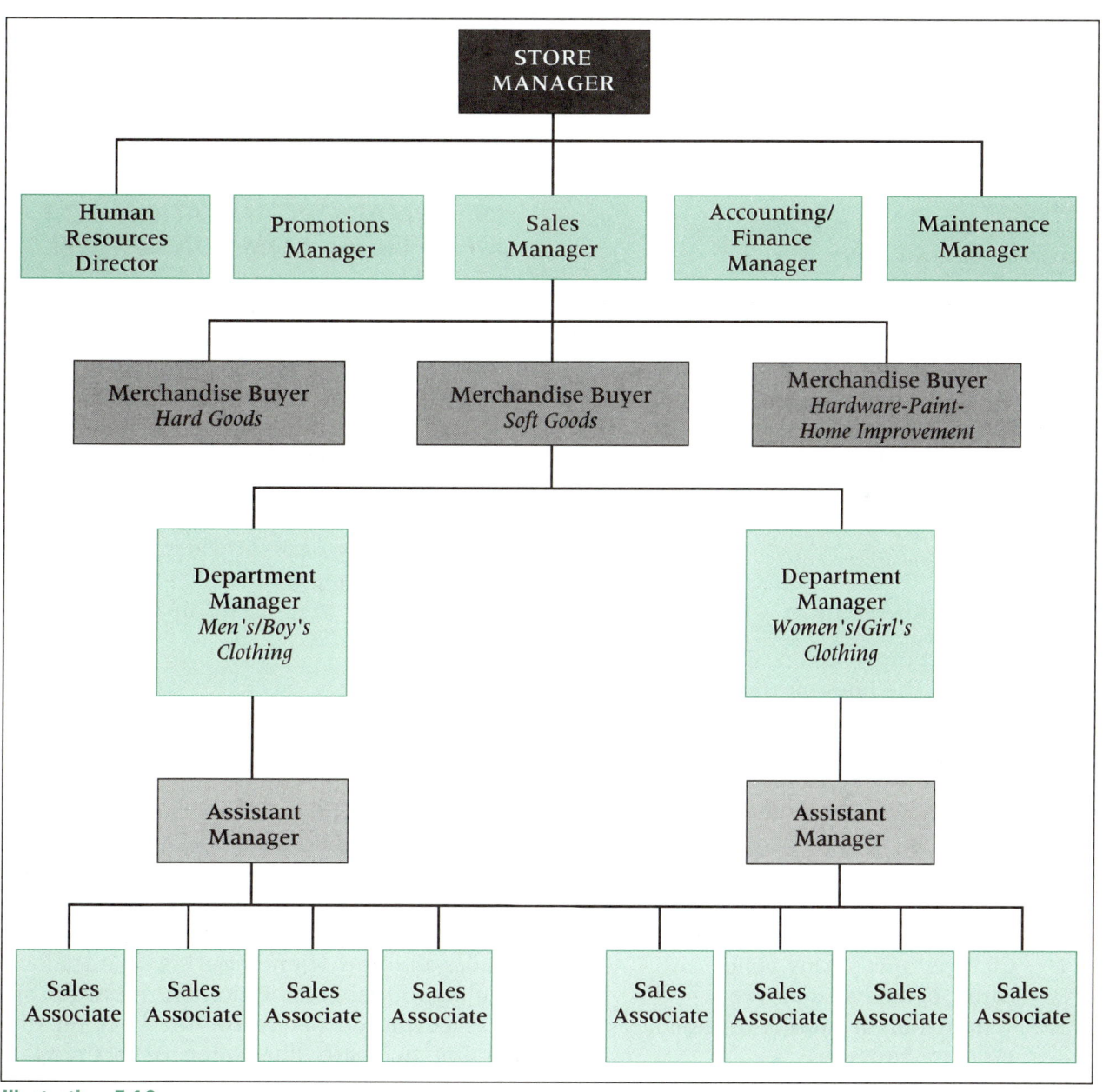

Illustration 5-10
Typical Department Store Organization Chart

```
          Store manager

  Human Resources, promotions,
   sales, accounting/finance, and
      maintenance managers

        Merchandise buyers

        Department managers

       Assistant department
            managers

             Sales
           associates
```

Illustration 5-11
People higher up in an organization have larger amounts of authority and responsibility.

of the triangle represents a small amount of authority and responsibility. Notice that the area becomes larger as it goes further up from the tip. This means that people higher up in the organization have larger amounts of authority and responsibility.

Lines of Communication

In the formal organization, lines of communication follow the lines on the organizational chart. For example, if the store manager in Illustration 5-10 decides to make a change in sales policy, notice of the policy change will flow down. In other words, official communication comes to an employee from his or her immediate supervisor.

Official communication from the top includes messages about the following matters:

1. Changes in company policy
2. Hiring of a new employee
3. Termination or transfer of employees
4. Working hours
5. Working schedules
5. Sales goals
7. Employee evaluations
8. Pay raises and promotions

It is possible that some co-workers may tell you about this or that communication. Until you hear the message from a supervisor or see it in writing, the communication is not official.

Official communications also flow upward. For example, a salesperson might have an idea on how to design a sales window display. The idea would be officially communicated upward, beginning with the salesperson's immediate supervisor. The salesperson does not go directly to the department manager or others higher in command. This would break the flow of communication and could result in leaving out important persons. The upward flow, like the downward flow, should be taken step-by-step.

INFORMAL ORGANIZATION FOR UNOFFICIAL COMMUNICATION

The *informal organization* refers to different groups at work that may be established because the members of these groups have something in common. For example, the members of a group may have a common social background, be of the same age bracket, have the same religion. These informal groups do not have formal authority. Yet the informal organization composed of these groups provides a system of informal communication. And sometimes this informal system may work more effectively than the formal one.

The Grapevine

The unofficial system of communication provided by informal groups is known as the grapevine. The term *grapevine* dates back to the Civil War in the United States. At that time, secret messages were sent over a telegraph line. This line was strung through trees and bushes almost like a vine. Today, the term *grapevine* includes all forms of unofficial communication.

Unlike official communication, messages on the grapevine do not follow the lines on the organization chart. Illustration 5-15 shows a partial organization chart. The solid lines represent the official lines of communication. The

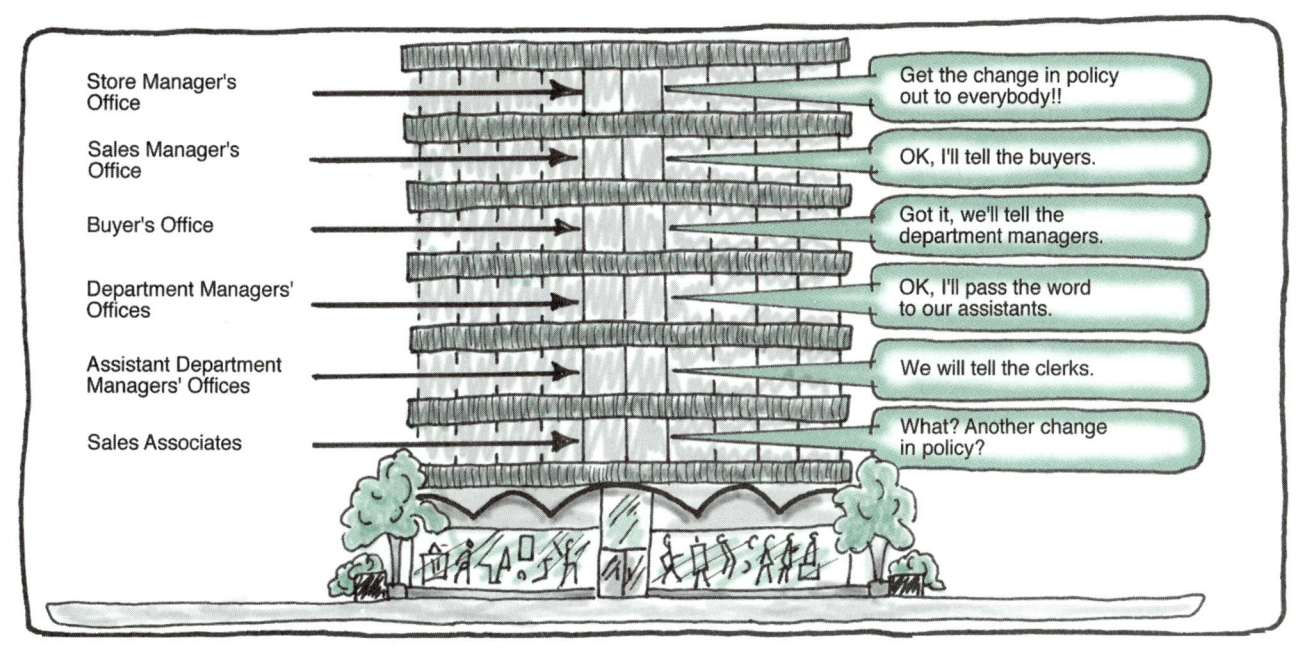

Illustration 5-12
Downward lines of communication.

broken lines represent the path taken by unofficial communication. Look at this chart and the unofficial lines of communication, and then read the next paragraph, which explains what took place.

Ruth overheard the store manager and the sales manager talking about changing the store hours. The store manager was thinking of keeping the store open until 9 p.m. on Thursday evenings. Then Ruth told Jake what she overheard. During lunch, Jake passed the same message to Lynn. Lynn then told all the other salespersons in the women's clothing department about it. As a result, Will asked Linda if he had to work on Thursday night. Linda didn't know what to say. She had special family responsibilities on Thursday nights and she began to worry about what to do. The rumor caused Linda and possibly her family, unnecessary stress and worry.

Is the Grapevine Accurate?

Those who conduct studies about informal communication suggest that the grapevine is about 80 percent accurate. This means that most messages passed along the grapevine are partially right. The problem is, which of the parts of the message are right and which parts are wrong? One small change in a message can alter the meaning of the entire message. Serious human relations problems begin when people assume that the grapevine is 100 percent right.

For example, let us take the case of Dean, an employee in a store. During an afternoon break, the store manager's secretary told Dean that the store would be closed tomorrow in order to hold the store's annual inventory. Last year the store was closed for a half day so that the

Illustration 5-13
Upward flow of communication

Illustration 5-14
The Grapevine

employees could take inventory of the goods. During the past two weeks, everyone at the store had been talking about the annual inventory. Dean was looking forward to that day because he could count the goods much more easily when he did not have to wait on customers. After his break, Dean told two of his co-workers to come to work tomorrow ready to take inventory. He simply told them what the store manager's secretary had said.

The next morning Dean and his two co-workers arrived at the store ready to take the inventory. They were all dressed casually for this purpose. On regular workdays they wore dress shirts and neckties. To their surprise, however, Dean and his co-workers found out that the store inventory would be taken that evening! Dean and his co-workers had to go home and change clothes.

Dean felt terrible, of course. He had caused problems for his two co-workers. Like Dean, they had to drive back home to change clothes. This took time and wasted energy. And Dean felt that he got them in trouble with the store manager. Naturally his co-workers were upset. The store manager was also upset because the store lost the sales that the employees would have made during the hour they were gone.

Dean had created a human relations problem by assuming that the grapevine message he heard was accurate. The truth is, the store manager's secretary omitted one small important detail from this message: *the taking of inventory was to be held at night*. Thus, her message was not complete. The secretary's message was only 80 percent right; 20 percent of the message was left out!

How Do Rumors Spread?

The grapevine sometimes has a bad reputation because it can spread rumors. A rumor is a widely spread story based on incomplete information. Some rumors may be true, and some may be false.

Rumors can be described by the following formula:

Rumor = Interest X Confusion

This formula states that a rumor depends on two factors: interest and confusion. The first factor has to do with the amount of interest a person has in the rumor. For example, a rumor about an employee marrying the boss might be of great interest to some employees, but not to others. A rumor about an employee getting

CHAPTER 5 ◆ INTERPERSONAL COMMUNICATION **135**

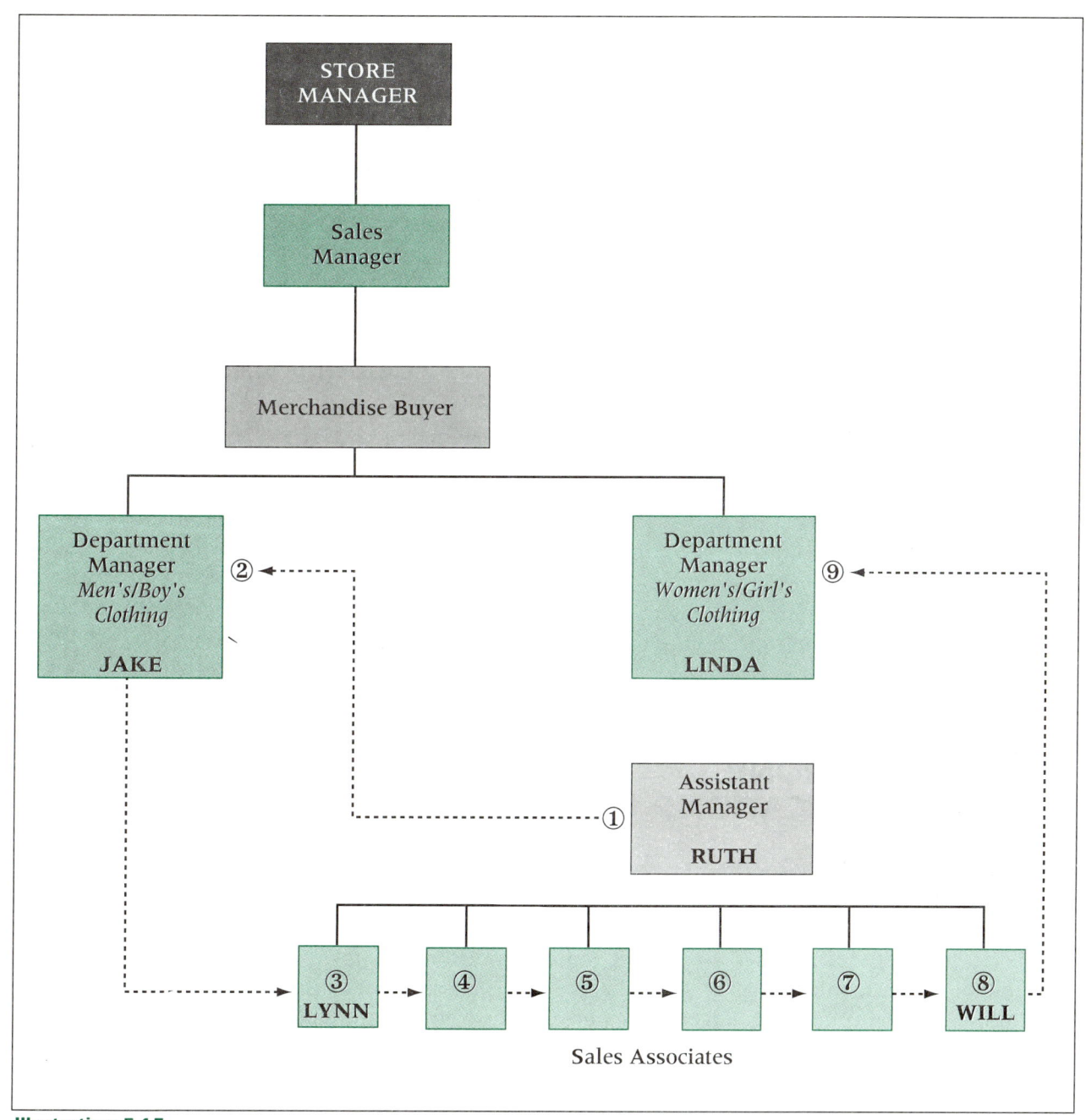

Illustration 5-15
The grapevine does not take the path taken by official communication.

fired may be of less interest to some than others. Rumors depend on high interest.

The second factor in the formula is confusion. This means that a message that is unclear may result in a rumor. The greater the lack of clarity, the more likely a rumor will result. For example, a story about an employee getting a traffic ticket for speeding could easily become a rumor. All it takes is for one person to tell the story with a few fuzzy details, as illustrated in following dialogue. Note how the lack of clear information adds to the rumor.

Bob to Sally: George got a ticket for speeding.

Sally to Harry: George was arrested for speeding.

Harry to Joan: The police got George for speeding.

Joan to Susan: I knew George would get in trouble; now he's in jail.

Rumors, like other messages on the grapevine, are usually about 80 percent accurate. However, if the message is highly emotional, its accuracy is reduced. For example, a rumor that the boss is being transferred may be slightly emotional, but the rumor that the boss's replacement plays favorites and is mean-spirited could be very emotional. Frightening stories about the new boss could spread quickly.

In summary, informal communication occurs every day. One cannot depend on messages from the grapevine to be accurate. Whenever possible, you should ask your supervisor about the accuracy of an informal message. The grapevine also carries rumors. Rumors are probably not true if the messages they carry are emotionally loaded. By understanding the limitations of informal communication, you will improve human relations at work.

ELECTRONIC COMMUNICATIONS

E-mail and voice mail communications are increasing daily. *E-mail* is a message typed on a computer and sent to a person or a group using an electronic network. The Internet is an example of an electronic network. A local area network, LAN, is another type of electronic network used to connect computers in an office or group of offices The widespread use of the Internet has made e-mail one of the most frequently used methods of communication.

Voice mail in its simplest form is a telephone answering machine. Most voice mail systems, however, do much more than record messages. Voice mail systems can send the same message to a list of people, and the sender just needs to say the message once. The system can be set to page you when you get a call that your answering systems records. Voice mail systems can also serve as storage places for messages. You can replay the message several days later if you wish. E-mail and voice mail are non-face-to-face electronic communications and are much different than regular face-to-face or voice-to-voice discussions. The ability of the sender to convey the appropriate tone and intent is more difficult with electronic communications. Overcoming these difficulties requires special communication methods and great sensitivity to human relations.

CHALLENGES OF NON-FACE-TO-FACE COMMUNICATIONS

E-mail and voice mail communications differ from face-to-face communications in our ability to get feedback and to clarify the message. Feedback may be verbal or nonverbal. Verbal feedback is the way we check for understanding of our message, usually by asking questions or listening to the person's response to our message. Nonverbal feedback also tells us if the receiver is getting the message correctly. Here, we look for head nods, smiles, or grunts of "uh huh" and similar sounds. Feedback that tells us the message is not understood, not appreciated, or generally not received may be immediately acted on to clarify the message. We can change the content and tone of the message quickly in order to enhance its meaning.

E-mail and voice mail do not have instant feedback features. Often the message is not acknowledged for several hours or even days. It is possible for e-mail to get lost and it's possible to unintentionally delete a voice or e-mail message. If the message was not understood as intended the negative consequences could be at best unfortunate and at worst damaging. Because of the risk of misunderstanding, great care must be exercised in sending electronic messages.

A good human relations rule to follow in sending e-mail or voice mail is not to send negative messages. The person receiving the message has no opportunity to clarify your intent or ask questions. You may get rid of some anger or bad feeling by sending a negative message—and you don't have to deal with the person's immediate reaction—but you will leave a semipermanent record of your bad feelings. If you call and get the person's voice mail, just leave a polite message requesting the person to call you regarding a problem. If it's e-mail, send a message asking for a face-to-face or voice-to-voice meeting to discuss a problem. Be extra careful to avoid accusing or blaming words. Keep your tone neutral and businesslike.

Here are some guidelines for e-mail. We have set them up using the FAQ *(frequently asked questions)* format common to electronic media.

FAQ: Sending and Receiving E-mail

Q: What goes in the subject line of e-mail?

A: The subject line and your name is all the receiver sees when receiving notice of an e-mail message. Make a good first impression with your subject line. It should be something that catches the attention of the receiver. Your message may be one of several messages. A good subject line will ensure your message gets read promptly.

Q: Should I use all UPPERCASE LETTERS in sending e-mail?

A: No, unless you want to appear to be talking LOUDLY. Uppercase is hard to read and using all capitals is considered impolite.

Q: I've heard e-mail is friendly and I don't have to worry about grammar and spelling.

A: Friendly doesn't mean sloppy. Do your best to use good grammar. Use your spelling check feature to help you avoid silly or embarrassing mistakes. Go easy on extra punctuation; a whole line of !!!!!! is boring. Some systems don't take quote marks (" "); the system software thinks they are special symbols. You may use arrows for quotes (>>blah blah<<).

Q: Is e-mail private? Can I send a very personal message?

A: E-mail is not private. The system administration group, that is, your online service help group, can read your mail. Others who might have access to your computer can read it. An embarrassing situation occurred when a person replied to a business e-mail with a very personal response. The e-mail software makes it very easy to reply. Just click on Reply, type your message, and click Send. Unfortunately, this software had two reply choices: Reply and Reply to All. The person thought Reply to All meant reply to all of the message. It meant, as our very embarrassed friend soon found out, send the reply to all (everyone) on the original message distribution list.

Electronics are not perfect. Even if correctly addressed, replies can also be misdirected. It's best not to put something in writing you would not want read by someone else.

Q: Can I sign e-mail?

A: Not in the same way you can sign a piece of paper. Your e-mail signature is usually a line or two with which you close your messages. Using the same closing ("Sincerely, The Boss") in all your messages creates your signature. You can also give your telephone and fax numbers as alternative ways to contact you.

Q: Some people get a lot of e-mail. Must you answer it all?

A: Some e-mail is like junk mail, advertisements and offers to sell things. Other e-mail is information, such as a message from the system administrator notifying you of system changes. And, other e-mail is in the form of a note or message to you. E-mail does not usually require a reply. You choose the messages to which you reply.

Q: I see a lot of abbreviations in e-mail. Where do I learn what they mean?

A: Keep abbreviations to a minimum, or others, may not understand what you mean. There are explanations of accepted abbreviations on the Internet. The most common ones are:

IMHO	In my humble opinion
FYI	For your information
BTW	By the way
ROFL	Rolling on the floor laughing
BCNU	Be seeing you
OOB	On or before
TTFN	Ta ta for now
TTYL	_____ (Can you guess it? Your teacher has the answer.)

Q: How can I show I am joking in an e-mail message?

A: Use the smiley face technique. With the keyboard colon, dash, parentheses, and other keys you can make smiley faces. Here are a few examples:

:-) smiley face on its side
:-(unhappy
:-> mischievous

_____ Can you make a smiley face wearing glasses? Wearing lipstick?

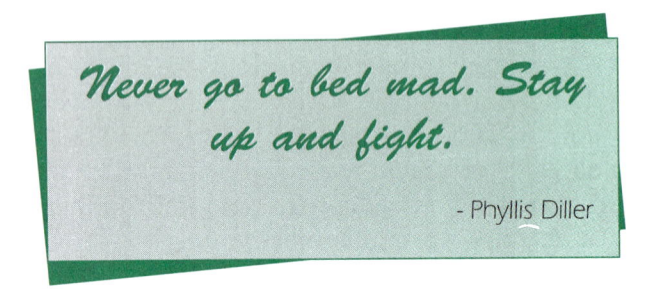

> *Never go to bed mad. Stay up and fight.*
>
> - Phyllis Diller

Sending and Receiving Voice Mail

Voice mail is very popular in organizations. It is fast, accurate, and can be used "7 by 24," that is, 7 days per week and 24 hours per day. Following are guidelines for effective use of voice mail:

- ◆ Keep messages short. Even though some systems allow up to three minutes of recording time for each message, try to keep your message to one minute or less.
- ◆ When leaving a message, give your name at the beginning of the message. You may leave your call-back number at the beginning with your name or at the end of the message.
- ◆ Do not leave negative or punishing messages of any kind. Discussions of this sort must be face-to-face or voice-to-voice.
- ◆ Change your voice mail greeting system daily. A permanent message that says, "Sorry I missed your call, please leave a message" is OK but it lacks sincerity. (At home, on your personal voice messaging system, permanent messages are more acceptable. Personal systems do not require professional standards.) At work, it is very easy to record a new message each day, such as: "Hi, this is John Public on Tuesday, March 1. Your call is important to me so please leave a message and I will get back to you."
- ◆ Do not use the voice mail greeting to detail your daily schedule. For example, it is not a good idea to say: "Hi, this is John Public, on Tuesday, March 1. I'll be in a meeting from 8 to 9:30 this morning; then I am out of the office until 2 p.m. You can reach me at 555-1212 during that time. From 3 to 5 p.m. I am in another meeting, and won't have a chance to return calls until after 5 p.m."

If you feel it is necessary to indicate you will not be available during the day, simply record a greeting that says: "Hi, this is John Public on Tuesday, March 1. I'll be out of the office most of the day. If you need to speak to someone right away, please call Jane Doe at 555-1211." Just be sure Jane is OK with the message.

- ◆ If you are connected to a voice mail network, learn to use it. It will have many sending and receiving features that can and will make your communications more effective and efficient than you might think. Most people who use voice mail regularly wonder how they ever got by without it.

CHAPTER 5 ◆ INTERPERSONAL COMMUNICATION **139**

CHECK YOUR UNDERSTANDING

To be sure you are reading and learning the key points, fill in the blanks with the missing word or group of words.

1. Give two reasons why people do not listen well.

_____

2. How could the way a speaker is dressed cause a listening problem?

_____

3. What is the difference between a fact and a feeling in a message?

_____

4. While listening to a person our minds may wander to some other place. What does a good listener do to recover?

_____

5. Give an example of official communication (a) flowing downward

_____

(b) flowing upward

_____

6. How accurate is the grapevine?

_____

7. State and explain the rumor formula.

_____

8. State two ways electronic communication is different from face-to-face communication.

_____

NET WORKING

Join us on the Internet. Check out our Human Relations for Career Success Home Page.

Try some of our special Internet Activities for Chapter 5. Your instructor will give you instructions on which activities would be good for you to complete.

Connect with us at:

http://success.swpco.com

Activity 5-1
UNDERSTANDING THE DEFINITION OF COMMUNICATION

The following projects will help you understand the first section of this chapter, "Definition of Communication."

1. Bring to class examples of the following:
   (a) A company magazine. What kind of information does the magazine communicate?

   _____
   _____
   _____
   _____
   _____

   (b) A company newsletter. What kind of information does the newsletter contain?

   _____
   _____
   _____
   _____
   _____

2. Interview three people by asking them this question: "How do you define good communication?" Write their answers in the following spaces. Then share your findings with the class.

Interviewee 1:
_____
_____
_____

Interviewee 2:
_____
_____
_____

Interviewee 3:
_____
_____
_____

Activity 5-1, continued

3. Draw a model below to illustrate the communication process. Use the model on page 135 in this chapter to help you get started. Try to include barriers to communication in your model.

4. Look up the following words in a dictionary. Then count the number of different meanings given for each word. Also indicate the most common meaning of each word. (It will be the first definition given.)

Word	Number of Meanings	Most Common Meaning of the Word
run	_____	_____
capital	_____	_____
common	_____	_____
tone	_____	_____
part	_____	_____

Activity 5-2
MEANINGS ARE IN PEOPLE, NOT IN WORDS

*T*his activity will help you understand why meanings are in people and not in words.
On the next page, write a story about a communication problem at school. Follow these directions carefully:

1. Notice that the next page has 25 lines on it. You begin the story by writing a sentence or part of a sentence on Line 1. Do not write on Line 2.

2. Tear out the page and give it to another person in the class, Person 2. The sentence written by Person 2 should continue the story you began.

3. Person 2 must now fold the paper so that the sentence you wrote on Line 1 cannot be seen.

4. Person 2 gives the paper to Person 3.

5. Person 3 reads only the sentence written by Person 2. Then Person 3 continues the story by writing on Line 3.

6. Person 3 must now fold the paper so that Lines 1 and 2 cannot be seen. Person 3 passes the paper to Person 4.

7. Person 4 may only read the sentence or words written on Line 3.

8. Other persons in the class should continue adding lines to the story in the same manner. Be sure that the paper is folded each time so that the next writer sees only the previous line.

9. After everyone in the class has written a line, read the story.

10. Was the story funny? How does the story illustrate the point that meanings are in people, not in words?

(Story sheet on following page.)

Activity 5-2, continued

1. _____
2. _____
3. _____
4. _____
5. _____
6. _____
7. _____
8. _____
9. _____
10. _____
11. _____
12. _____
13. _____
14. _____
15. _____
16. _____
17. _____
18. _____
19. _____
20. _____
21. _____
22. _____
23. _____
24. _____
25. _____

Activity 5-3
UNDERSTANDING WHAT ALLNESS IS

Your teacher will need several volunteers. If you do not choose to be a volunteer, complete the Observer part of this activity.

This activity requires that you listen carefully. When you have completed this activity, you will have a better understanding of allness. Your teacher will provide the directions for this activity.

To the Volunteers

Form a circle with your desks in the center of the room. The teacher will give each of you an envelope. Open your envelope and read the directions in it. After you have read the directions, begin your discussion.

To the Observers

You have a special job during this activity. You must take notes about the discussion. Use the next page to write your notes. Listen for allness statements that the role-players make. When you hear words such as **always**, **never**, and **every time**, write what was said on the note page. Refer to page 120 for a review of allness.

Allness Statements by Volunteer 1:

_____
_____
_____
_____
_____

Allness Statements by Volunteer 2:

_____
_____
_____
_____
_____

Allness Statements by Volunteer 3:

_____
_____
_____
_____
_____

Activity 5-3, continued

Allness Statements by Volunteer 4:

Allness Statements by Volunteer 5:

Allness Statements by Volunteer 6:

Activity 5-4
LISTENING FOR EMOTIONALLY LOADED WORDS

Two student volunteers are needed for this activity. One student will role-play a company manager. The other student will role-play an employee. By completing this activity, you will learn about the dangers of emotionally loaded words.

Role of Manager

You are the manager of Company Z. You must discipline an employee who came to work late for the third time. The employee also dresses inappropriately. This carelessness hurts the company. Use emotionally loaded words as you talk to the employee. Review emotionally loaded statements on page 124 before you begin.

Role of Employee

You are to react to the manager as you think the employee would react. Disagree and show signs of tension.

The maximum time allowed for this activity is five minutes. The teacher will, if possible, tape-record the conversation. After the conversation, the teacher will play back the tape. The tape will be stopped every few sentences so that everyone can list the emotionally loaded words or sentences in the conversation. Use the next page to write your list.

After the taped conversation ends, write a less emotionally worded script of the conversation opposite the emotionally loaded script in your list.

Then answer the following questions:

1. How did the employee react to the emotionally loaded words? Describe the employee's reaction.
   _____
   _____
   _____
   _____
   _____

2. Explain the difference between a positive tone and a negative tone. Which do you prefer?
   _____
   _____
   _____
   _____
   _____

Activity 5-4, continued

3. Is a negative approach ever justified? When?

4. Did you hear any statements of allness? If so, what were the statements?

5. Did labeling occur? If so, give examples.

6. List two ways to avoid emotionally loaded words. How can you apply the two ways to the discussion between the manager and the employee?

Emotionally Loaded Words or Sentences	A Better Way to Say the Message

Activity 5-5
LISTENING FOR FACTS AND FEELINGS

This activity will help you learn to listen for feelings as well as facts. Remember that most people can get the facts in a message. It is more difficult to listen for feelings. Keep this formula in mind as you take part in this activity:

Message = Facts + Feelings

Four student volunteers are needed to put on a demonstration debate for the class. Two student volunteers will support the issue, and the other two will oppose it. Each pair of debaters will attempt to influence the class to either agree or disagree with the following statement:

> Anyone who works hard for a living should be required to support others who fail to provide for themselves.

The class may think of other issues to debate, but the one selected should contain a judgment based on feelings and opinions.

To the Volunteer Debaters

Each debater has two minutes to argue for or against the issue. Try to separate fact from opinion. Use both logic and emotion to support your points. Follow this schedule for your debate:

Speaker	Purpose
1	support
2	oppose
3	support
4	oppose

After the debate is concluded, the audience should be polled to see how many agree and how many disagree with the issue debated. The members of the class will be asked to explain why they voted as they did.

1. What problems come up when the opposing side forgets to listen for feelings?
   _____
   _____
   _____
   _____
   _____

2. Why is it difficult to get agreement on value statements?
   _____
   _____
   _____
   _____
   _____

Activity 5-5, continued

3. How often did the opposing side mistake feelings for facts?

4. Why is it more difficult to find proof for value statements than for statements of fact?

5. What communication barriers arise when false opinions and feelings get in the way of listening?

6. Did the audience let their own sentiments and attitudes affect the way they heard the arguments?

Activity 5-6
THE WRONG TIME TO COMPLAIN

This activity is designed to help you study the formal organization. By completing this worksheet you will learn how to communicate effectively through the formal organization.

> ### Case Study
>
> Chad was very happy on Tuesday morning. He went on his morning break with Charlie, the supervisor of the furniture department. Chad wanted to get transferred to the furniture department. While the two were drinking their coffee, Mr. Barnes, the store manager, sitting at a nearby table, called out: "Come over here, Charlie, I want to talk with you." Charlie then said, "Come on, Chad, let's go sit with the boss."
>
> Chad sat quietly while Charlie and the store manager talked. After about five minutes, Chad decided to get into the conversation. Chad said, "You know, Mr. Barnes, I sure would like to sell furniture. I think I could sell furniture. At least I could sell it better than I sell those stupid toys!" Charlie then said, "Well, Chad, we'll talk about it." Chad replied, "Yes, I sure would like to talk about it."

1. Why did Charlie seem to avoid further talk about Chad's desire to be transferred?

_____
_____
_____
_____
_____

Activity 5-6, continued

2. What do you think Mr. Barnes thought about Chad's actions?

   _____
   _____
   _____
   _____

3. What is the proper way to apply for a transfer to another department? Use the organization chart shown on page 131 in this chapter to help you answer this question.

   _____
   _____
   _____
   _____
   _____

Activity 5-7
CHOOSING ALTERNATIVES TO SEXIST LANGUAGE

Following is a list of words and phrases. Select the words that are sexist and write the reason why the word or phrase is prejudicial. Then write an alternative word or phrase that is nonsexist.

Example: The term **manpower** is sexist because it assumes that workers are men. An alternative gender neutral word is **workforce**.

Sexist Language*	Reason Why It Is Prejudicial	Alternative Word or Phrase
anchorman		
female lawyer		
manhole cover		
male nurse		
manicurist		
repairman		
secretary		
stewardess		

*Hint: Some words in this list may **not** be prejudicial.

6 Self-Development

Knowledge

After reading this chapter, you will be able to:
- Define the term *self-image*.
- Compare and contrast inner- and other-directed people.
- Analyze strategies that enable people to gain self-knowledge.
- Illustrate the valuing process and apply the process to values at work.
- Define *justice* and discriminate between the three levels of practicing justice.

Attitudes

After reading this chapter, you will:
- Want to develop a positive self-image.
- Accept the ideals of the inner-directed person.
- Value self-knowledge.
- Judge issues and problems using higher-level concepts of justice.

Self-esteem is the total of all you believe about yourself. It may be determined by your answers to the following questions:
- Who are you?
- What is important to you?
- Do you like yourself?
- Where are you going in life?

In this chapter we will study self-development beginning with the most important relationship you have—the relationship you have with yourself. We also will work on finding what values are important to you. The last two of these questions will be covered in the next chapter.

WHO ARE YOU?

How much do you know about yourself? Before you answer this question, try answering how you would describe yourself:

- to a friend
- to a teacher
- to your parents
- to your supervisor at work
- to yourself

Do you realize that you might describe yourself differently depending on the situation? Everybody does this; some do this more than others. Ideally, you describe yourself in the same manner to everyone.

People describe themselves differently to different people for many reasons. The two main reasons are: (1) people have many selves, and (2) people try to put the best combination of their many selves forward.

YOUR MANY SELVES

You have many selves. For example, you may have:

- a friendly self
- a romantic self
- a selfish self
- a modest self
- an honest self
- a clever self
- a curious self
- an assertive self

awesome... ...romantic
outgoing... ...attractive
cold... ...hardworking
proud... ...smart
nervous... ...cranky

Illustration 6-1
Your many selves.

Any one of these selves may be a part of a description of you. Your own private definition of these selves is your *self-image*. In a way, your self-image is what you think of yourself. To get an idea of what you think of yourself, try rating yourself on the various scales shown in Illustration 6-2. Each scale ranges from 1 to 10. The highest rating is 10, the middle rating is 5, and the lowest rating is 1.

Each rating is a definition. The definition is what you mean by friendly, honest, greedy, and the like. The definition is personal. It is what you think of yourself. It is your self-image.

If you were to rate these different selves tomorrow, would the ratings change? The ratings might change because your moods do affect the way you feel about yourself. On the average, however, your ratings of yourself remain the same.

PUTTING ON YOUR BEST SELVES

When you are with someone, you try to put the best combination of your many selves forward. Understanding how you decide which selves to make known to others is important. By being aware of how such decisions are made, you can help yourself answer the question, Who are you?

People decide which of their main selves to reveal to others by four different methods. These are (1) by doing what others expect, (2) by doing what others prescribe, (3) by acting on trial and error, and (4) by acting on personal beliefs. Each of these methods will be illustrated in this chapter. The use of each method will tell whether a person's behavior is other-directed, other- and inner-directed, or inner-directed.

Method 1: Doing What Others Expect

When you talk with others, what you say and the way you act may be a result of what they expect from you. Bill is a person who does what others expect. He works after school

Illustration 6-2
Self-Image Rating Scale

My Friendly Self

10	9	8	7	6	5	4	3	2	1
very friendly				generally friendly					not friendly

My Honest Self

10	9	8	7	6	5	4	3	2	1
always honest				usually honest					dishonest

My Greedy Self

10	9	8	7	6	5	4	3	2	1
not greedy				somewhat greedy					very greedy

My Modest Self

10	9	8	7	6	5	4	3	2	1
always modest				middle of the road					boastful

and on weekends in a warehouse. His job is to load and unload trucks. The employees at the warehouse use crude language when they talk. Sometimes they complain about the poor working conditions in the warehouse. Bill joins in and swears with them because he believes they expect this from him.

At home Bill doesn't use foul language because he knows that his parents expect him not to swear. And when Bill is with his friends, he tends to brag slightly about his warehouse job because he thinks his friends expect him to be proud of his job. After all, he has the best-paying job among them.

Bill does what others expect him to do. People like Bill, who gear their behavior to what others expect, are other-directed people.

Illustration 6-3
Rating your self-image.

Illustration 6-4
Does the job applicant represent an inner-directed or other-directed person?

Method 2: Doing What Others Prescribe

In this method, people decide "by prescription" which of their selves to project. Generally, a prescription is an order for medicine based on a physician's diagnosis. The prescription is taken to a pharmacy, where medicine is obtained. When the medicine is taken by the person who is ill, that person usually recovers.

Taking someone's advice is like taking a prescription. You know that advice is coming when you hear people say:

- Why don't you . . .
- If I were you, I'd . . .
- If you were smart, you'd . . .
- When are you going to . . .
- Here is what you ought to do . . .
- You might want to consider . . .

Can you think of other ways people lead up to giving prescriptions? Write your answer in the spaces below.

_____
_____
_____
_____
_____
_____
_____

People who depend on others to tell, advise, and prescribe actions for them are also other-directed persons. Sally is an example of such a person. Sally constantly asks her co-workers what she should do. "Should I trade in my car? Should I go out with Jim? Should I change my printer cartridge? Should I go on a diet? Should I ask for a raise?" Sally finds security in asking others what to do. She is comfortable being a puppet whose actions are controlled by others.

People like Sally seek out prescriptions so that they don't have to think for themselves. To them, taking advice or prescriptions from others is safe. If another person's prescription does not work, it is not her fault. Sally and people like her fool themselves by thinking that such a failure rests with the person giving the prescription. The person simply gave poor advice. The receiver of the prescription then looks for a new prescription. By following this procedure, advice-seekers need never take responsibility for their own actions.

Method 3: Acting by Trial and Error

A person who uses the trial-and-error method in putting his or her best foot forward is continually experimenting. Carlos uses this method. When he isn't sure about something, he tries to figure out the situation. Then he gives himself a prescription. For example, Carlos believes that he is particularly good at figuring out his teachers. His class schedule reads like this:

- First period: No sweat, just talk a lot in class.
- Second period: Be cool, write a bunch on the test.
- Third period: OK, I'm on the team.
- Fourth period: Act tough, talk loud.
- Fifth period: Teacher's a pushover; she likes boys more than girls.

Illustration 6-5
Doing what others expect.

Carlos uses what he knows about his teachers to make decisions. If something doesn't work, Carlos tries another tactic. If Carlos's next idea is unsuccessful, he tries something else. He tries to find out what others want or like. When he thinks he knows, he tries to get the other person to make life easy for him. Carlos watches the reactions of others very carefully. He must do this because his next move depends upon the reaction of others. People like Carlos are other- and inner-directed people.

Method 4: Acting on Personal Beliefs

An inner-directed person decides which self to put forward by acting on personal beliefs. These personal beliefs are logical and unemotional. The inner-directed individual asks the questions: With which of my selves am I most comfortable? With which of my selves am I most successful? This person then reveals the most logical combinations of these selves.

The actions of inner-directed people are based on what they believe. They do not put up false fronts. They are not manipulated or used by others, and they don't manipulate or use others. Because inner-directed people present the same set of selves to others most of the time, they are genuine. People who experience lasting success in their personal lives or at work are inner-directed persons.

Stacy is an example of an inner-directed person. She knows which of her many selves she likes best. She also knows which is most successful. Stacy presents the same set of selves to her supervisor, her co-workers, her parents, and her friends.

For example, Stacy believes that getting an associate's degree from a nearby community college is important. She plans to enroll in this college next year. Although her parents do want her to go on to college, several of Stacy's friends and relatives have different opinions on the subject. Some of Stacy's friends see no

Illustration 6-6
An inner-directed person acts on personal beliefs.

future in going to college. Her supervisor at the store where she works graduated from a university and thinks that an associate's degree won't be worth much. Stacy's grandparents don't want her to attend the local community college because many of their friends sent their children to expensive private colleges. Finally two of Stacy's co-workers quit college after a year; they think that Stacy won't make it through college either. So, Stacy feels a lot of pressure on this subject.

To ease the pressures surrounding her, Stacy could use any one of the three methods already described. How do you think Stacy would use the following methods to adjust herself to this situation? Write your answers in the spaces provided.

Using Method 1 (doing what others expect), Stacy could:

Tell her supervisor:

_____
_____
_____
_____
_____

Tell her friends:

_____
_____
_____
_____
_____

Using Method 2 (doing what others prescribe), Stacy could:

Tell her co-workers:

_____
_____
_____
_____
_____

Using Method 3 (acting by trial and error), Stacy could:

Tell her grandparents:

_____
_____
_____
_____
_____

But Stacy does not use any of these three methods of revealing her many selves. Stacy bases her actions on personal beliefs. She does not argue with people. She does not agree with people just to be agreeable. When asked her opinion of her plans, Stacy states what she believes. She makes the same statement to everyone. When others give opposite views, Stacy tries to understand why. Sometimes, of

Action Based On	Person Described As	Result of Action
What others expect	Other-directed	Chameleon effect
What others prescribe	Other-directed	Puppet effect
Trial and error	Other- and inner-directed	Manipulation effect
Personal beliefs	Inner-directed	Genuine effect

Table 6-1
Summary of other- and inner-directed behavior.

course, Stacy changes her views. Just because she has given her opinion about something does not mean that she cannot change her mind later on. However, when Stacy changes her mind, she does not try to hide it from certain people.

You must realize, however, that Method 4—acting on personal beliefs—is difficult to adopt. It's hard to continually be logical, unemotional, and confident that any decision made is sound.

The four methods of revealing yourself to others, and the results of these methods, are summarized in Table 6-1.

Learning More about Yourself

How do you find out more about yourself? Generally there are two ways people learn about themselves over a lifetime: (1) by luck, and (2) by conscious effort.

Learning by Luck

Learning about oneself by luck is characteristic of immature people. Such people go through their lives not knowing much about themselves. They wonder why they did something. They wonder why others react to them in certain ways. But they never try to find out. When these people do learn something about themselves, it is often through plain luck.

Learning by Conscious Effort: The Johari Window

Increasing your self-knowledge requires some effort. To begin this effort, you must give and receive information about yourself. This giving and receiving process is shown in Illustration 6-7. The illustration is called the Johari Window because it was developed by Joseph Luft and Harry Ingham.

The Johari Window is like a picture of your personality. It represents four sections: (1) the arena, (2) the hidden section, (3) the blind spot, and (4) the unknown section.

The Arena. The arena section of your Johari Window represents information about you that you know and most of your friends know. Notice the headings "Things I Know" and "Things Others Know" for the upper left block in Illustration 6-7.

On the next page are two examples of information about you which, if true, would be known to you and to most of your friends. Try to add two more examples.

	Things I Know	Things I Don't Know
Things Others Know	Arena	Blind Spot
Things Others Don't Know	Hidden	Unknown

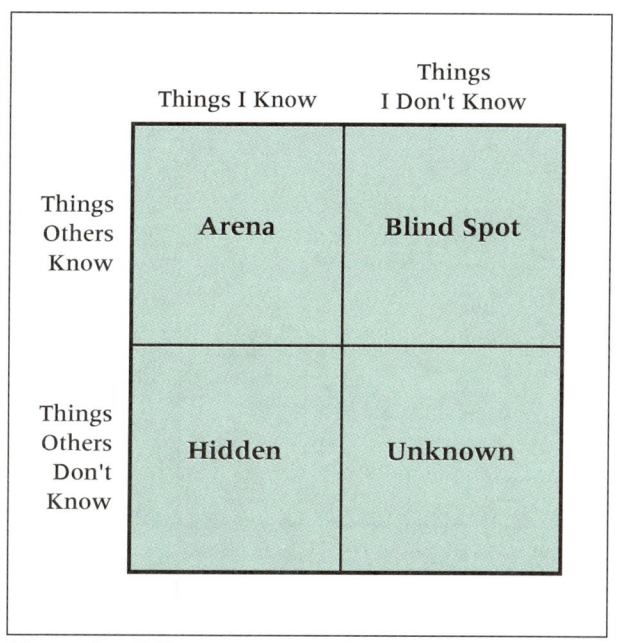

Illustration 6-7
The Johari Window

Things I Know

Things	1. I work at a TV station.
Others	2. I have two brothers.
Know	3. _____
	4. _____

The Hidden Section. The hidden section of your Johari Window contains information about you that you know, but no one else knows. This information is private. However, if someone asks you, you might give it.

Here are two examples of private or hidden things. Try to add two more.

Things I Know

Things	1. I secretly want to own my
Others	own business.
Don't	2. I enjoy being with my
Know	cousins.
	3. _____
	4. _____

The Blind Spot. The blind spot of your Johari Window contains information about you that you do not know, and the interesting aspect of this section is that others know this information about you. For example, you may cough before you speak or you may curl your hair with a finger while you talk. The point is that others know this but you are not aware of doing it.

The Unknown Section. The unknown section of your Johari Window represents the unconscious. This means that neither you nor anyone knows about the information on you in this section. For example, this section may contain memories from your early childhood. It also represents unexplored abilities. For example, some day you could be a great salesperson, but for now you have no idea that the ability to be a great salesperson is in you.

USING YOUR SELF-KNOWLEDGE

When you know yourself, you have a Johari Window that looks like Illustration 6-8.

Notice that the arena in Illustration 6-8 is the largest section of the window. This means that you freely give and receive information about yourself. Other people see you as honest and trustworthy because most of your behavior is open and straightforward. People do not have to guess about your intentions.

When your Johari Window has a large arena, this also means that you have much self-knowledge. The more self-knowledge you have, the better you understand who you are. And when you understand yourself, you can understand others better.

Understanding other people is essential to good human relations. Whenever you judge someone, you use yourself as the point of reference. For example, Mrs. Summers, a restaurant manager, asked Lisa, the assistant manager, about Tim's ability to serve customers. "Is Tim fast at taking food orders at the counter windows?"

When Lisa commented about Tim, she used herself as the measuring device. She thought to herself: "Tim is about as fast as I am. Joe is much slower than I. And Tim is definitely faster than Joe." So she said, "Why, yes, Mrs. Summers, Tim is pretty good at window service."

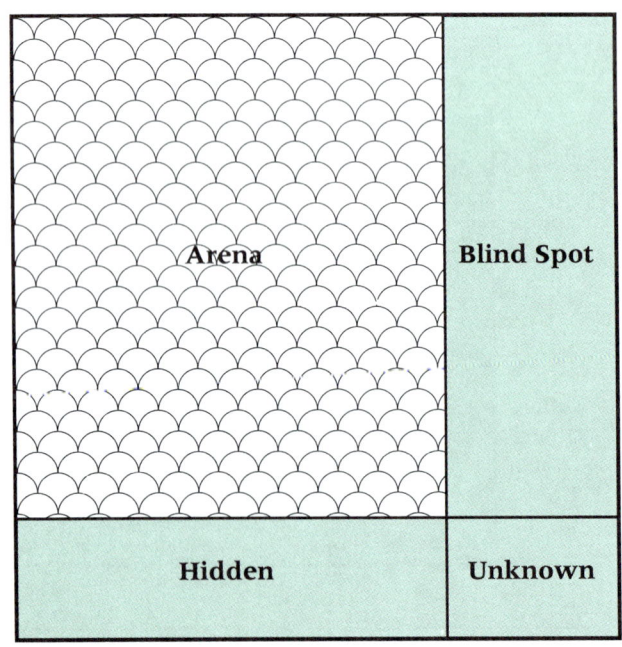

Illustration 6-8
The Johari Window of a person with much self-knowledge.

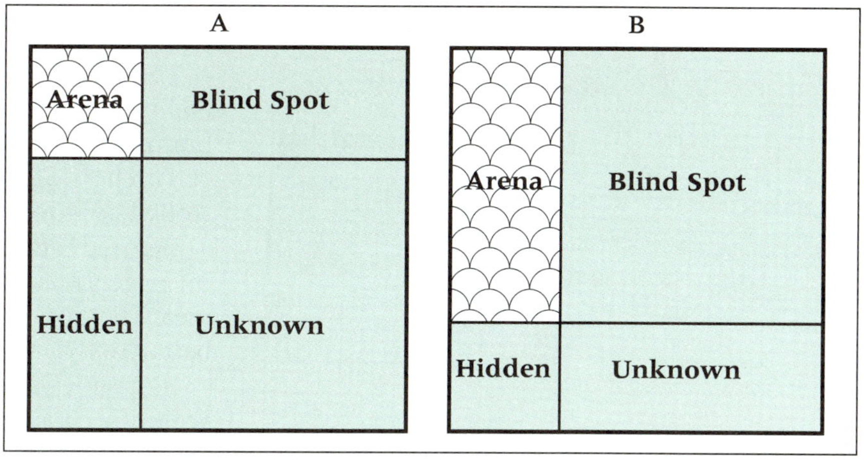

Understanding yourself is especially important when personal feelings are involved. Suppose Mrs. Summers asked Joe, rather than Lisa, the same question. Joe may be jealous of Tim, so his answer may be affected by his feelings. However, if Joe has some self-understanding, he may think to himself: "Yes, Tim is pretty fast. He is so fast that he makes me look slow. It's kind of embarrassing. I could say he's just OK at the windows. Or I could say he's fast because we do all the cleaning up for him while he takes orders from customers. That's partly true. Oh well I might as well admit it. Tim is pretty good at the order windows."

Joe is aware of his negative feelings for Tim. Joe also knows why, but he doesn't try to hide it from himself with excuses. Joe understands himself. Which of the two Johari Windows in Illustration 6-9 do you think belongs to Joe?

If you answered B, you are correct. Window B has the larger arena. At the end of this chapter, you will find a questionnaire that will enable you to plot your own Johari Window. By filling out the questionnaire, you can measure your self-knowledge and then use it to understand yourself and others better.

Illustration 6-9
Which is Joe's Johari Window?

CHECK YOUR UNDERSTANDING

To be sure you are reading and learning the key points, fill in the blanks with the missing word or group of words.

1. What is self-image? _____

2. How many selves do you have? _____

3. Match the method on the left to the statement on the right:

Method 1
Doing what others expect

Method 2
Doing what others prescribe

Method 3
Acting by trial and error

Method 4
Acting on personal beliefs

___ Asking with which of my selves am I most comfortable?

___ Experimenting, figuring it out

___ Acting on others' advice

___ Other-directed

___ Chameleon effect

4. Things I know and things others know is referred to as the _____.

5. A person with little self-knowledge has a Johari Window with a large _____.

> *We are what we repeatedly do. Excellence, then, is not an act, but a habit.*
>
> - Aristotle

BRAIN DOMINANCE THEORY

Learning by conscious effort also includes being aware of your behavior traits. For example:

- Do you like to be on time, and are you upset if others are not on time?
- Do you like to initiate conversation, or do you let others start a discussion?
- Are you good at planning, but not so good at following through with the details of the plans?

The answers to these questions may be related to your brain orientation.

The Discovery of Two Sides of the Brain

The study of brain orientation is often referred to as *brain dominance theory*. Brain dominance means that the way you think and behave depends on which side (or hemisphere) of your brain is the more influential. This theory is based on the fact that the human brain has two sides, and each side operates independently. The discovery of "independent sides" was made by Dr. Roger Sperry in the early 1960s. For his work, Dr. Sperry received a Nobel Prize in 1981.

Other scientists and doctors used Sperry's discovery in their own work. Many of these scientists began studies to find out which side of the brain performed certain tasks. They found that the *left* side of the brain controls the right side of the body, and that the *right* side of the brain controls the left side of the body.

Left- and Right-Brain Behavior

The *left* side of the brain controls speaking ability for most people. The *right* side of the brain controls humor and emotion. Yet, not all researchers agree on which behaviors are controlled by the left or the right side of the brain?[1]

Before reading further, complete Activity 6-5 on page 185. That activity may give you some idea of your brain orientation and associated behaviors.

Behavior patterns have been discovered from scientific classification of tasks performed by the left or the right side of the brain. These behaviors, and the side of the brain responsible for them, are summarized in Illustration 6-10.

Use the information on brain dominance to help you understand behavior tendencies. If you tend to be left-brained yourself, you may be uncomfortable in relationships with those who are right-brained. Similarly, those with a strong right-brain orientation may be uncomfortable with those who are left-brained. Knowing this, you can learn to value people with strengths that are the opposite of yours. Many effective work teams have members with left- and right-brained dominance. Each member then makes up for the deficiencies in other members. The result is a well-balanced team.

It is important to note that neither a left- nor a right-brain orientation is better than the other. The most desirable orientation is one that is balanced. This is referred to as *whole-brain thinking*.

WHAT IS IMPORTANT TO YOU?

Everyone has values. *Values* are personal beliefs that tell you what is desirable and worthwhile. Values also tell you what is right or just. Your values help you decide what is important and help you determine what choices to make in your everyday life. When you are at work, you must make value judgments.

---

[1]. Ann Gibbons, "New Maps of the Human Brain," Science (July 13, 1990), pp. 122-123.

Illustration 6-10
Behaviors associated with the left or right hemispheres of the brain.

Left Brain — Specialist: logical, detailed, organized, familiar, controlled, structured

Right Brain — Generalist: intuitive, holistic, unorganized, unfamiliar, emotional, spontaneous

To get a better idea of what values are, complete the following sentences:

◆ I'm for . . . . _____
_____

◆ I'm against . . . . _____
_____

◆ On Friday night I usually . . . . _____
_____

◆ On my day off work I like to . . . . _____
_____

◆ I enjoy reading about . . . . _____
_____

The statements you wrote say something about you. The statements indicate some of the things you believe are or are not worthwhile or desirable.

THE VALUE SYSTEM

Just as everyone has lungs and a heart, everyone has a personal value system. The value system works by processing thoughts and ideas—some are used, and others are thrown away. Those thoughts and ideas that are used by a person become his or her values. All value systems work the same way, but the thoughts and ideas that become values are different from one person to another.

How People's Values Are Different

To show you how values differ, try to answer this question: How long is a long time? Write your answer in the space below.

Answer: A long time is _____
_____

Now compare your answer with the answers of your classmates. Are there many different answers? There are probably as many answers as there are students in the class.

Try another one: How many people live in a small town?

Anwer: _____ people live in a small town.

Again compare your answers with those of your classmates. How many people had the same answer? (Probably not very many.)

Here is one more: When is a person successful?

Answer: A person is successful when _____
_____
_____ .

Discuss your answer to success with others in class.

Illustration 6-11
How much money is a lot of money?

Factors That Affect Values

Values differ because of the many factors that affect the formation of values. Table 6-2 shows a list of some of these factors. Look at the list and ask yourself:

- Which people affect my values?
- Which places affect my values?
- Which things affect my values?

How the Value System Works

Illustration 6-12 is a diagram that shows how the value system works. Look at this diagram and note that the starting point of the value system is an idea. All ideas are connected to one or more of three sources. The three sources are: people, places, and things.

People includes parents, relatives, friends, neighbors, teachers, employers, and co-workers. *Places* includes the part of the country in which you live or have lived in the past. Places also includes the size of the town or city in which you live (or have lived). The type and size of the school you attend (or have attended) are also a part of places. *Things* means radio and TV programs, movies, books, tapes, compact disks (CDs), videocassettes, newspapers, magazines, computer games and software, and so on. All of these things are sources of ideas for you.

Ideas and Self-Image. Your value system processes ideas (about people, places, and things) and combines them into a possible value. This means that the idea is not a value at this stage; it is still just an idea. The first question that comes to your mind is, Does the idea fit my self-image?

There are three possible answers to this question. These are:

1. The idea fits my self-image.
2. The idea does not fit my self-image.
3. The idea does not fit my self-image, but it might be worth considering; and I can change my self-image a little.

If the idea fits with your personal definition of you, you may or may not wish to try on the idea. If the idea does not fit your self-image and you have no desire to give it further consideration, you forget the idea. However, if you think the idea is worth considering even though it does not fit your self-image, you must be prepared to change your self-image.

For example, William plays the guitar in a country music band. Recently, he met a successful musician who plays classical music.

PEOPLE	PLACES	THINGS
Parents	Countries in which you have lived	Radio
Friends	Part of the country in which you live (have lived)— North, South, East, West	TV, VCR
Employer(s)		Movies
Co-workers		Books, magazines
Relatives		Newspapers
Neighbors	Part of town where you live	Tapes, CDs
Teachers	Schools you attend	Computers
Members of the community	Places you visit	

Table 6-2
Factors that affect values.

CHAPTER 6 ◆ SELF-DEVELOPMENT **167**

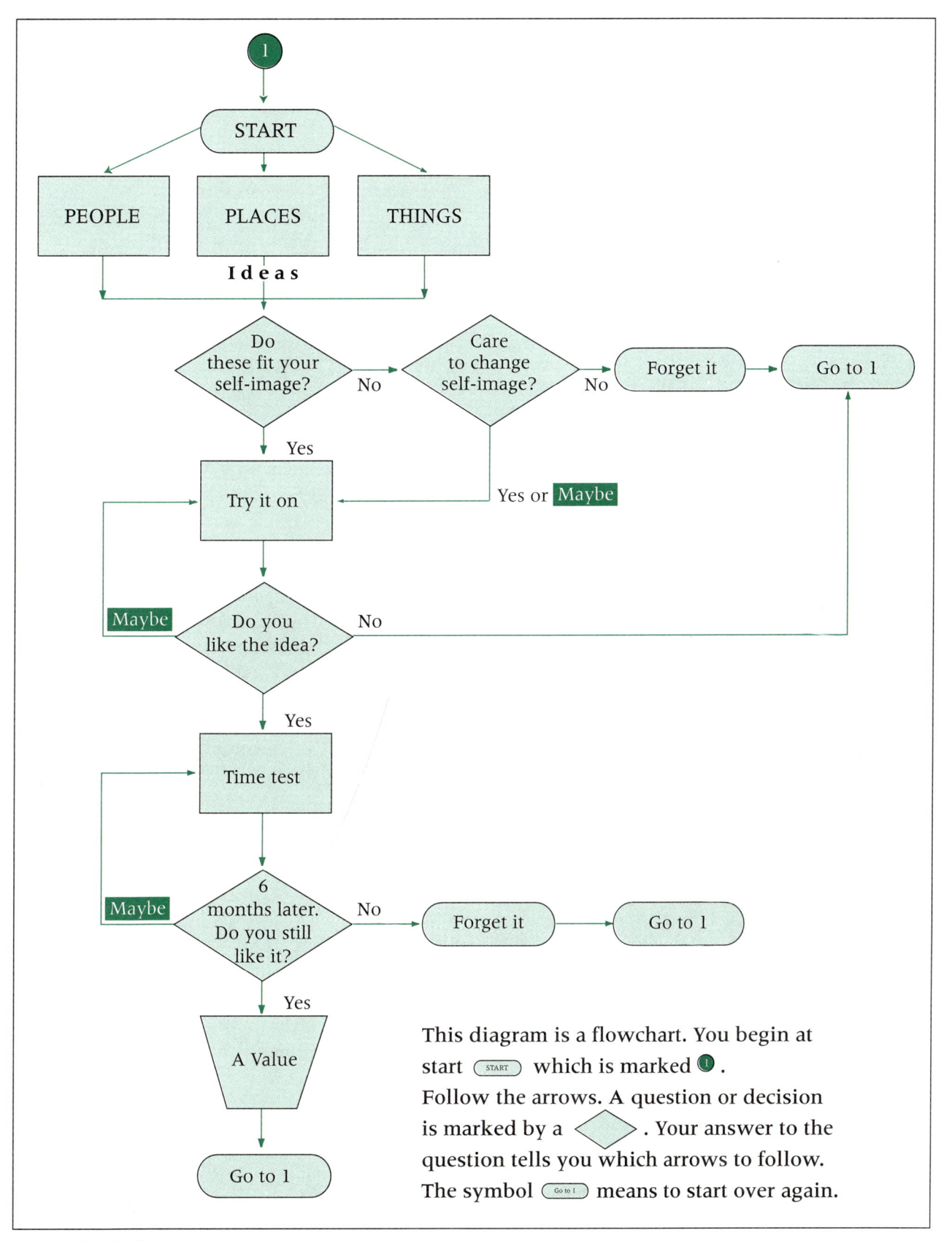

```
                        ①
                         ↓
                    ┌─────────┐
          ┌─────────│  START  │─────────┐
          │         └─────────┘         │
          ↓              ↓              ↓
     ┌────────┐    ┌────────┐     ┌────────┐
     │ PEOPLE │    │ PLACES │     │ THINGS │
     └────────┘    └────────┘     └────────┘
          │         I d e a s           │
          │              ↓              │
          │         ╱────────╲          │
          │        ╱    Do    ╲         │
          │       ╱ these fit your ╲ No    ╱────────╲              ╭──────────╮         ╭──────────╮
          │       ╲  self-image?  ╱────→ ╱   Care   ╲ No           │ Forget it│ ──────→ │ Go to 1  │
          │        ╲            ╱       ╱to change  ╲ ──────────→  ╰──────────╯         ╰──────────╯
          │         ╲──────────╱        ╲self-image?╱
          │              │ Yes           ╲         ╱
          │              ↓                ╲───────╱
          │         ┌──────────┐               │ Yes or [Maybe]
          └────────→│ Try it on│←──────────────┘
                    └──────────┘
                         ↓
              ╱──────────╲
   [Maybe]   ╱   Do you   ╲   No
    ┌──────╲   like the   ╱──────────────────────────────────────→
    │       ╲    idea?   ╱
    │        ╲──────────╱
    │             │ Yes
    │             ↓
    │        ┌──────────┐
    └───────→│Time test │
             └──────────┘
                  ↓
              ╱──────────╲
   [Maybe]   ╱     6     ╲
    ┌──────╲ months later.╱ No       ╭──────────╮        ╭──────────╮
    │       ╲Do you still╱──────────→│ Forget it│ ─────→ │ Go to 1  │
    │        ╲  like it? ╱           ╰──────────╯        ╰──────────╯
    │         ╲──────────╱
    │              │ Yes
    │              ↓
    │         ╱──────────╲
    │        ╱  A Value   ╲
    │        ╲────────────╱
    │              ↓
    │         ╭──────────╮
    │         │ Go to 1  │
    │         ╰──────────╯
```

This diagram is a flowchart. You begin at start ⬭START⬭ which is marked ①.
Follow the arrows. A question or decision is marked by a ◇. Your answer to the question tells you which arrows to follow. The symbol ⬭Go to 1⬭ means to start over again.

Illustration 6-12
How the value system works.

After this meeting, the idea of listening to classical music—Bach, Chopin, and Beethoven—came to William. Because his self-image about music is to be a little different, the idea of listening to classical music fits with William's self-image.

Suppose another idea comes to William—the idea of joining a group that plays classical music. This idea is too different and does not fit with his self-image. Furthermore, William does not choose to change his self-image about country music. Therefore, William forgets this idea.

Trying on the Idea. If an idea fits your self-image, you may wish to try it on. Even if the idea does not fit your self-image, you may want to try it on if you don't mind changing your self-image. Trying on the idea is the next step in the value system. It means actually doing something with the idea.

Let us go back to William's idea of listening to classical music. Suppose he decides that this idea fits his definition of himself and he cares to change his self-image. This means that the idea is still alive and has a possible value. William tries on the idea by beginning to listen to some classical music.

Illustration 6-13
William is listening to classical music.

Once you have tried on an idea, the next question is, Do I accept the idea? The three possible answers are:

1. Yes.
2. No.
3. Maybe.

If your answer is yes, you may wish to give this idea the time test. If your answer is no, the flowchart of the value system in Illustration 6-12 indicates that you can go back to the beginning and consider another idea. If your answer is maybe, the flowchart indicates to try it on again. In other words, keep trying the idea for a while.

After listening to classical music for some time, William can make a decision. If he does not like the idea, he forgets it. If his answer is maybe, he decides to keep listening to classical music for a while longer. Then he asks the question again, Do I like the idea? If William's answer is yes, the idea is ready for the time test.

The Time Test. If an idea is to become a value, it must last. The time test takes about six months. Any time before six months pass, your value system may classify the idea as a fad. A *fad* is an interest that is only temporarily popular. Clothing styles, hairstyles, restaurants, athletic clubs, cute or clever gifts, and TV programs, to list a few, can be faddish. That is, they are very, very popular for a short period of time.

If after six months you are still unsure of the idea, your value system will continue the time test.

Accepting the Idea as a Value. If you like the idea a year after you first considered it, the idea becomes a value. This value is now a definite part of you. It permanently helps you decide not only what is desirable and worthwhile, but also what is right and just.

VALUES RELATING TO JUSTICE

All problems that require decisions about what is right relate to justice. What is right may also be called what is just. Every day people who work in businesses must make decisions

Illustration 6-14
Ed's concern for Scott's physical power makes him decide to return the money.

about what is just. Values help people make judgments about what is right.

For example, everyone agrees that stealing is wrong. But suppose a man steals medicine to save his child's life. He steals the medicine because he does not have enough money to buy it from a pharmacist who refused to sell the medicine at a lower price. Should this man be put in jail for stealing to save his child's life? How would you decide the answer in this situation? This part of the chapter will help you understand values about justice and how to decide what is right in a given situation.

When deciding what is right, people base their decisions on one of three motives: (1) concern for power, (2) concern for rules and orders, and (3) concern for human rights. Sometimes a person will use a combination of these three motives, but the decision is always based on one or more of them.

Concern for Power

Concern for power is about physical and nonphysical power.

The use of physical power means "might makes right." A person using physical power to decide what is right says, "You either do what I believe is right or you will be punished." The neighborhood bully often behaves this way. Wars are fought and terrorists try to impose their will on others because of the belief that physical power will decide who is right.

Take the example of Scott and his younger brother, Ed. Both of them worked at a convenience food store. Scott saw Ed take $10 from the cash register and put it in his pocket. During their morning break, Scott told Ed that he saw him take the money and warned him to put it back or else he would beat up Ed. Ed knew that Scott would beat him up, so Ed decided to put the money back in the cash register. But just before Ed put the money back, he offered to split it with Scott—$5 each. Scott refused and just shook his fist at Ed.

The second part of concern for power is nonphysical. In this case, justice is defined as, "You scratch my back and I'll scratch yours." This means that, if you do me a favor, I will pay you back with a favor. Whether you like the person or not is unimportant.

Concern for Rules and Orders

When people practice justice because of their concern for rules and orders, they do so because they respect rules and the authority that makes the rules. People who use this reason believe that it is their duty to follow rules or orders without exception. This reason also encourages

Illustration 6-15
Alice is persuading Mary to follow rules and orders.

people to do the right thing only because it pleases others.

For example, Mary was driving her sister Alice home one night after work. Mary had her lights on the high beam so that she could see down the road. As a car approached from the opposite direction, Mary did not switch her lights to the low beam. Alice asked Mary why she didn't switch the lights. Mary said she didn't think of it. Alice then told Mary that it was courteous and polite to switch to a low beam so that the other drivers could see better. In this situation, Alice was trying to persuade Mary to do the right thing because "nice people do behave this way."

A short time later, another car passed and again Mary did not dim her lights. This time Alice told Mary that the state's driving laws required her to dim her lights whenever a car passed in the opposite direction. In this situation, Alice was trying to persuade Mary to dim her lights based on the need to follow rules and orders.

Concern for Human Rights

The concern for human rights is a reason that is based on both written and unwritten laws. The Bill of Rights in the Constitution of the United States is an example of written laws that support this reason. Here justice means what is right for everyone in the world. When a person bases a decision on concern for human rights, he or she places respect for individuals above blind obedience to authority and to written rules.

For example, Todd is a high school student who works part time. He needed a good used car to drive to work and school. So he went to a used car lot. He explained to the salesperson just what he needed and how much he could afford to pay each month. After looking at several models, Todd narrowed his decision to two cars. Both were of similar quality, but one cost $700 more than the other. The more expensive car was a little more attractive in style. Todd would have preferred this car, but he knew he

> *No one can make you feel inferior without your consent.*
>
> - Eleanor Roosevelt

would have very little money left because of the higher monthly payment on a loan to buy it. So he chose the lower-priced car.

Now Roger, the salesperson, knew that he could use the bigger commission on selling the higher-priced car to pay his bills. Besides, Roger had orders from the car lot owner to sell as many higher-priced cars as possible. Furthermore, Roger knew that he could talk Todd into buying the more expensive car.

However, Roger believed that Todd's needs would be served very well by the lower-priced car. This way Todd would have some money left from his paycheck for other things. Roger also believed that, even though it would be in the immediate interest of the car lot owner and himself to sell the more expensive car, it would be morally wrong to do so. Roger knew that the professional salesperson helps the customer select the right product for his or her needs. Everyone won because Roger took the right action. Todd got a car that matched his needs, Roger prepared himself for a long-term customer relationship with Todd, and the car lot's reputation in the community was maintained.

When you make decisions about what is right, try to use concern for human rights to help you make these decisions. By doing this, you will improve your relations with the people involved in these decisions.

MANAGING BY VALUES

Effective managers of businesses or organizations manage by values. This means that such managers know:

1. What is important to themselves and to those who work with them.
2. What is good for the business or the organization.
3. How to decide what is right based on a concern for human rights.
4. How to apply this knowledge to their day-to-day actions.

Here are some value statements that some managers use to guide their decision making:

- Conduct business affairs with integrity.
- Confront and constructively resolve any incident of disrespect.
- Encourage innovation and creativity when solving problems.
- Be a profitable growth company.
- Treat all employees as individuals without regard to race, gender, or physical disability.

For managers, as for anyone, choosing or deciding is much easier when values are clear. If you are a manager or intend to be one, consider practicing "Superman" or "Superwoman" management. These comic book characters believed in "truth, justice, and the American way." At work, "Superman" or "Superwoman" management means

1. We never lie to ourselves or to our customers.
2. We treat one another and our customers fairly.
3. We provide a product or a service at a competitive price.

CHECK YOUR UNDERSTANDING

To be sure you are reading and learning the key points, fill in the blanks with the missing word or group of words.

1. List three characteristics of
   - the left side of the brain:
     _____
     _____
     _____
   - the right side of the brain:
     _____
     _____
     _____

2. What is whole-brain thinking?
   _____
   _____
   _____

3. What is a fad? How does it relate to the value system?
   _____
   _____
   _____
   _____

4. Insert the letter of the motive on the left next to the statement on the right where you think it applies:

   a. Concern for power
   b. Concern for rules and order
   c. Concern for human rights

   ___ Nice people do this
   ___ Do this or be punished
   ___ What is right for all
   ___ Blind obedience
   ___ Do me a favor

NET WORKING

Join us on the Internet. Check out our Human Relations for Career Success Home Page.

Try some of our special Internet Activities for Chapter 6. Your instructor will give you instructions on which activities would be good for you to complete. Connect with us at:

http://success.swpco.com

Activity 6-1
RIDDLE OF THE SPHINX

This activity is designed to help you learn more about others. It also gives you the chance to tell about yourself. The title, "Riddle of the Sphinx," comes from the ancient play Oedipus Rex by Sophocles. Giving the answer to the riddle assured one would not be eaten by the sphinx. Here is the slightly modified riddle:

> What in the spring moves on four feet,
> In the summer moves on two feet, and
> In the fall moves on three?
> The more feet it moves,
> The weaker it be.

Many an unsuccessful traveler guessed nearly every type of animal, bird, or insect. Only Oedipus got it right. If you want to guess, stop here and look away from the page. The answer comes next.

The correct answer to the riddle is a human. We move as babies by crawling on all fours; the reference to spring is to the beginning of life. We move upright on two feet as we mature, our summer. We move on three feet in old age, the fall season. The third foot is a cane or crutch.

Directions:
Draw three pictures in the spaces provided on the next page:

Spring:
Picture things that were important to you as a child. What people, places, and things do you see?

Summer:
Picture what is important to you as a maturing person. For example, what would your ideal job and ideal vacation be?

Fall:
Picture other people asking you for advice. Who are they and what are they asking about? What are you doing?

Artwork isn't important. Make your drawings as brief or as detailed as you wish. Be sure that they contain enough information to answer the questions.

Share your spring, summer, and fall with the class. Explain the meaning of your picture for each season.

Illustration 6-16
The Sphinx in Egypt.

174 HUMAN RELATIONS FOR CAREER SUCCESS

Activity 6-1, continued

SPRING

FALL

SUMMER

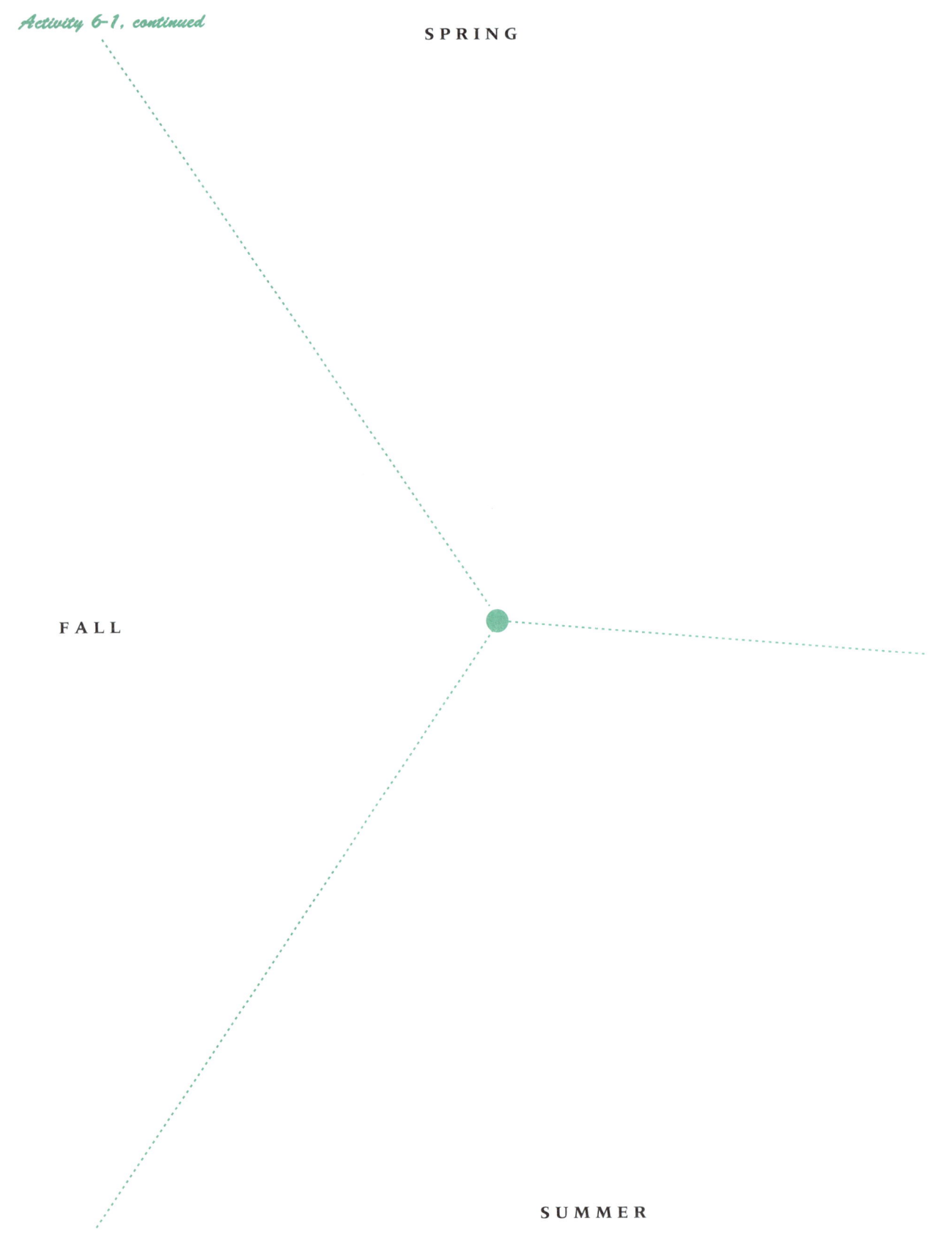

Illustration 6-17
The seasons of your life.

Activity 6-2
METHODS OF REVEALING YOUR MANY SELVES

The questions in this activity refer to the four methods used to decide which of your many selves to put forward. In the spaces provided, write an answer to each question listed.

1. Method 1: Doing what others expect.
How can you tell what:
  a. Teachers expect?

  b. Friends expect?

  c. People at work expect?

2. Method 2: Doing what others prescribe.
  a. What is a prescription? Give an example.

  b. Has anyone given you a prescription recently? If so, what was it?

  c. Have you given anyone a prescription recently? If so, what was it? Did the person specifically ask for this kind of direction?

  d. How do you feel when you get a prescription that you didn't ask for?

  e. Do prescriptions help people? Are there dangers in relying on prescriptions?

Activity 6-2, continued

3. **Method 3: Acting by trial and error.**
   a. Carlos, the young man in the example on page 158 of this chapter, uses Method 3. Describe Carlos or a person that you know who uses Method 3.

   b. Do students use Method 3 with their parents? If so, give an example.

   c. Do parents use Method 3 with each other? If so, give an example.

   d. Do employees use Method 3 on their supervisors? If so, give an example.

4. **Method 4: Acting on personal beliefs.**
   a. Are people who practice Method 4 inner- or other- directed?

   b. What is the main difference between an inner-directed and an other-directed person?

   c. What does it mean to be logical and unemotional?

   d. Should people be logical and unemotional at all times?

   e. How do you know when your actions are based on your personal beliefs?

Activity 6-3
THE JOHARI WINDOW

This activity will enable you to plot your own score sheet for your Johari Window. First, follow these directions:

1. Read the words in Columns I and II on this page.
2. Decide which of these words best describe you.
3. Circle the ten words in Column I and the ten words in Column II that best describe you.
4. After you circle the words that best describe you, have three other friends in your class do the same in describing you. Have your friends use Worksheets 2, 3, and 4 on the next three pages.

WORKSHEET 1

Completed by _____

WORDS THAT BEST DESCRIBE ME

Column I	Column II
accepting	aloof
biased	candid
critical	clever
curious	closemouthed
helpful	direct
inexperienced	frank
innocent	guarded
insensitive	noncommittal
joking	observant
judgmental	obstinate
keen	outspoken
modest	private
nosy	risk-taking
persistent	shy
questioning	silent
receptive	sly
searching	straightforward
sincere	tactful
strong-willed	unselfish
trusting	yielding

Total Points for Column I = _____

Total Points for Column II = _____

Activity 6-3, continued

WORKSHEET 2

Completed by _____

WORDS THAT BEST DESCRIBE MY FRIEND

Column I

accepting
biased
critical
curious
helpful
inexperienced
innocent
insensitive
joking
judgmental
keen
modest
nosy
persistent
questioning
receptive
searching
sincere
strong-willed
trusting

Total Points for Column I = _____

Column II

aloof
candid
clever
closemouthed
direct
frank
guarded
noncommittal
observant
obstinate
outspoken
private
risk-taking
shy
silent
sly
straightforward
tactful
unselfish
yielding

Total Points for Column II = _____

Activity 6-3, continued

WORKSHEET 3

Completed by _____

WORDS THAT BEST DESCRIBE MY FRIEND

Column I

accepting
biased
critical
curious
helpful
inexperienced
innocent
insensitive
joking
judgmental
keen
modest
nosy
persistent
questioning
receptive
searching
sincere
strong-willed
trusting

Total Points for Column I = _____

Column II

aloof
candid
clever
closemouthed
direct
frank
guarded
noncommittal
observant
obstinate
outspoken
private
risk-taking
shy
silent
sly
straightforward
tactful
unselfish
yielding

Total Points for Column II = _____

Activity 6-3, continued

WORKSHEET 4

Completed by _____

WORDS THAT BEST DESCRIBE MY FRIEND

Column I

accepting
biased
critical
curious
helpful
inexperienced
innocent
insensitive
joking
judgmental
keen
modest
nosy
persistent
questioning
receptive
searching
sincere
strong-willed
trusting

Total Points for Column I = _____

Column II

aloof
candid
clever
closemouthed
direct
frank
guarded
noncommittal
observant
obstinate
outspoken
private
risk-taking
shy
silent
sly
straightforward
tactful
unselfish
yielding

Total Points for Column II = _____

Activity 6-3, continued

SCORING YOUR TEST

1. Your teacher will read the words that receive answer points. Add up the points in each column on the four work-sheets. Then place your scores in the spaces provided at the bottom of the worksheets.

2. Illustration 6-19 is an example of a plotted score. In this example the total points are as follows:

Scores from Worksheet 1
Total Points, Column I = 20
Total Points, Column II = 30

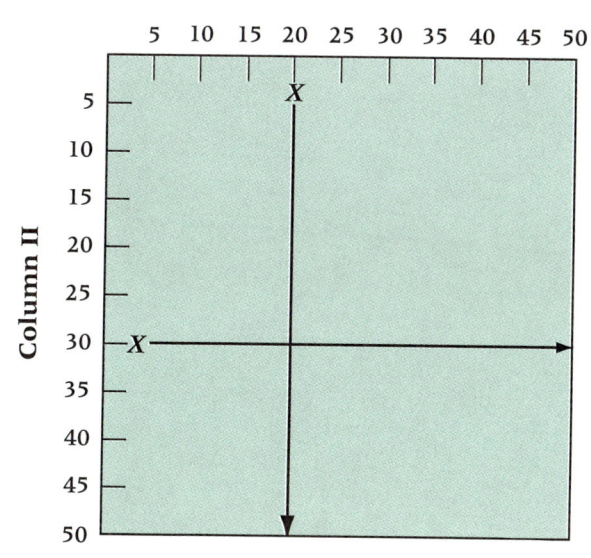

Illustration 6-18
Example of a plotted curve.

The person who plotted Illustration 6-18 placed an X on the top horizontal line of the square by the number 20 and also placed an X by the number 30 on the left vertical line of the square.

3. Plot your score. Then place your X's on the top and left sides of the square in Illustration 6-19.

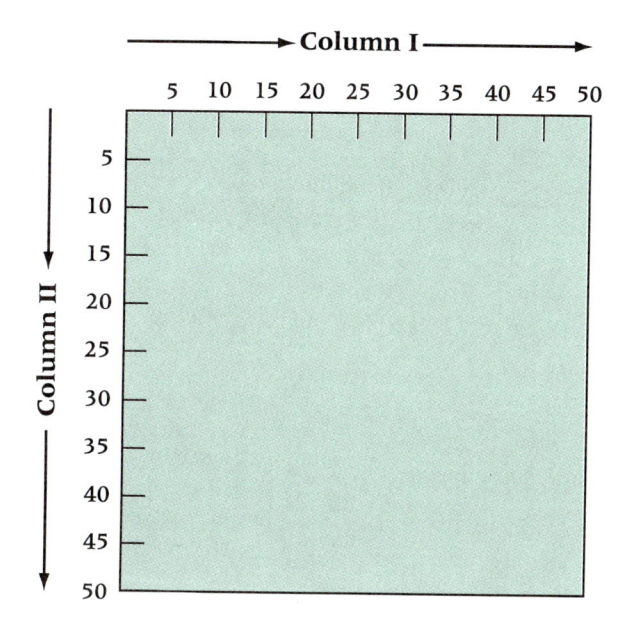

Illustration 6-19
My Johari Window—how I describe myself.

Make your Johari Window by drawing straight lines through the X's across the square and down the square, as shown in Illustration 6-19.

4. Now plot your score in Illustration 6-20 (on the next page) from the three worksheets completed by your three friends. Your score equals the sum of the points from each column, divided by 3. For example:

	Col. I	Col. 2
Scores from Worksheet 2:	20	25
Scores from Worksheet 3:	15	35
Scores from Worksheet 4:	25	30
Total Points	60	90
Total Points Divided by 3	60/3	90/3
YOUR SCORE	**20**	**30**

Activity 6-3, continued

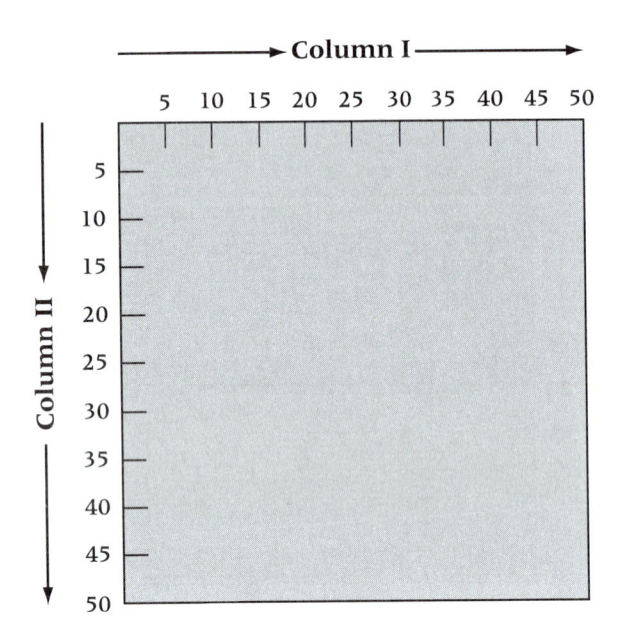

```
            ──────► Column I ──────►
            5  10  15  20  25  30  35  40  45  50
         5 ┤
        10 ┤
        15 ┤
   C    20 ┤
   o    25 ┤
   l    30 ┤
   u    35 ┤
   m    40 ┤
   n    45 ┤
  II    50 ┤
```

Illustration 6-20
My Johari Window—How others describe me.

Activity 6-4
DISCUSSION OF THE JOHARI WINDOW

Answer the following questions in the spaces provided.

1. How can a person with a large blind spot decrease the blind spot and increase the arena?

_____
_____
_____
_____
_____
_____

2. How can a person with a large hidden section decrease the hidden section and increase the arena?

_____
_____
_____
_____
_____
_____
_____

3. How can a person with a large un-known section decrease the unknown section and increase the arena?

_____
_____
_____
_____
_____
_____

Activity 6-5
BRAIN ORIENTATION QUESTIONNAIRE

Read the following statements carefully. Then, using the Response Key given below, CIRCLE the responses to the right of the statements that best match your preferences.

Response Key:

SA	=	strongly agree
A	=	agree
D	=	disagree
SD	=	strongly disagree

1. I am usually on time. **SA A D SD**
2. I like to try new fads. **SA A D SD**
3. Winning is important **SA A D SD**
4. I like a lot of space. **SA A D SD**
5. I prefer to read slowly. **SA A D SD**
6. I play a musical instrument. **SA A D SD**
7. I am good at math. **SA A D SD**
8. I am quick to decide things. **SA A D SD**
9. I tend to go back to the same restaurants. **SA A D SD**
10. I should be more serious. **SA A D SD**

The Scoring Sheet and directions on how to interpret your score are given on the following page.

Activity 6-5, continued

Statement #	SA	A	D	SD
1	1	2	3	4
2	4	3	2	1
3	1	2	3	4
4	4	3	2	1
5	1	2	3	4
6	4	3	2	1
7	1	2	3	4
8	4	3	2	1
9	1	2	3	4
10	4	3	2	1

Sum of the numbers circled: _____

Interpret Your Score:

IF: THEN:
The total score is: The dominant brain orientation is:

10 to 20 — Left Brain
21 to 30 — Balanced
31 to 40 — Right Brain

Activity 6-6
LOOKOUT MOUNTAIN

A group of tourists went on a sightseeing tour. The tour bus stopped on top of Lookout Mountain. After taking some pictures and walking through some abandoned mine shacks, Cora and her boyfriend, Jim, returned to the bus loading area. The bus was gone. It had left accidentally without them. Jim became very upset, for he had left his medicine on the bus. Without the medicine he becomes very ill. In fact, he began to feel ill immediately. Cora wanted to help Jim, so she went to see Lou.

Lou operated the small restaurant on top of the mountain. He owned an old car that Cora hoped he would use to take her to the bus to get Jim's medicine. Lou agreed, provided that Cora would steal the cellular telephone from the bus and give it to him. Cora refused. She went to Bert, the only other person on the mountain.

Bert was an old miner who lived in a shack behind the restaurant. Cora told him her problem. Bert said he could not help her and that she herself must decide what is right or wrong. Cora decided that she had no choice. She went back to the restaurant. She told Lou she would do as he asked.

When Cora and Lou returned, Cora ran happily to Jim with the medicine. He took it and began to feel better. Then Cora told Jim what she had done. Jim was shocked at her behavior! He told her he never wanted to be seen with her again.

The tour bus returned the next day. While waiting for the bus to leave, Cora told her friend Abe what happened. Abe felt sorry for Cora. Therefore, when Jim came along to get on the bus, Abe grabbed him and beat him up.

1. Rank the people in the story from first place to fifth place in the spaces provided. Assign the first place to the person you like best. Assign the fifth place to the one you like least. Place the other persons in the middle according to how much you like them.

   1st place _____

   2nd place _____

   3rd place _____

   4th place _____

   5th place _____

2. Explain your choice for first place.

_____

_____

_____

_____

Activity 6-6, continued

3. Which persons are using the "You scratch my back, I'll scratch yours" reasoning? How do you know?

___

4. Which persons are using punishment as a method of reasoning? How do you know?

___

5. Did Jim act the way he did because of blind obedience to rules or laws? Explain.

___

6. Assume that you want to convince someone that Bert should be in first place. What will you say in order to convince that person?

___

Activity 6-7
A GROUP DILEMMA

This activity involves a group discussion problem. Form groups of five people and discuss the following problem:

A nuclear disaster has ended. The only human beings alive are ten people in a bomb shelter. It will take six months for the radiation to drop to a safe level. The supplies in the shelter can barely sustain six people for the six months.

What should they do?

The ten people in the bomb shelter are the following:

1. Susan S., age 60, a history professor.
2. Roe R., age 28, a movie star.
3. Pat K., age 40, a police officer.
4. Kay M., age 21, an Olympic gold medal winner.
5. Lyn P., age 42, a scientist.
6. Marie G., age 34, a physician.
7. Ken B., age 28, a mechanic.
8. Maria B., age 28, the mechanic's pregnant wife.
9. Fr. Jackson, age 36, a priest and civil rights activist.
10. Joe M., age 19, a migrant worker.

After your group has decided on a strategy, please complete the following statements about what you learned.

"I Learned" Statements

1. I learned that I
_____
_____
_____

2. I realized that I
_____
_____
_____

3. I relearned that I
_____
_____
_____

4. I noticed that I
_____
_____
_____

Activity 6-7, continued

5. I discovered that I
_____
_____
_____

6. I was surprised that I
_____
_____
_____

7. I was displeased that I
_____
_____
_____

8. I was pleased that I
_____
_____
_____

Activity 6-8
VALUES PAST, PRESENT, AND FUTURE

What were the values of your ancestors? What will be the values of your descendants? What is really important today? This activity will help answer these questions and clarify your own values. The activity is divided into three parts. Your teacher will give you additional directions and help in completing each part.

Part 1

Ten value items are listed on the next page. Based on your values, which is most important? which is next in importance? Rate the items in this way: give 10 points to the most important item, 9 points to the next most important item, and so forth, until finally 1 point is given to the least important item. Write your answers in the "Today" column of the ranking sheet.

Part 2

This part of the activity will help you get ready to think about the values of the past and the values of the future. Answer the following questions. A written answer is not necessary. Just think of answers and share them in a brief class discussion.

A. 500 Years Ago

1. What were the most common forms of government?
2. What kinds of jobs did people have?
3. What technology (tools) existed to improve the quality of work life and/or personal life?
4. What did people do for entertainment? Where did they go for entertainment?
5. What was the average length of life? Why?

B. 500 Years Ahead

1. What will be the most common forms of government?
2. What kinds of jobs will people have?
3. What technology (tools) will exist to improve the quality of work life and/or personal life?
4. What will people do for entertainment? Where will they go for entertainment?
5. What will be the average length of life? Why?

Now turn the page over to complete this activity by filling in your value ranking sheet.

Activity 6-8, continued

Part 3

Your teacher will give you directions for completing this part of the activity.

TIME TRAVEL VALUE RANKING SHEET

ITEM	TODAY	500 YEARS AGO	500 YEARS AHEAD
Helping sick and disadvantaged people	_____	_____	_____
Physical appearance you are happy with	_____	_____	_____
Good friends	_____	_____	_____
Long, healthy life	_____	_____	_____
Happy marriage	_____	_____	_____
Career success	_____	_____	_____
Enjoyment of nature and the environment	_____	_____	_____
A beautiful home	_____	_____	_____
Financial security	_____	_____	_____
Good judgment	_____	_____	_____

7 Becoming a High Achiever

Knowledge

After reading this chapter, you will be able to:
- ✓ Describe a relationship between high achievement and self-confidence.
- ✓ Identify characteristics of high achievers.
- ✓ Write short- and long-term goals.
- ✓ Define the term **priorities**.
- ✓ Describe the process of making trade-offs.

Attitudes

After reading this chapter, you will:
- ✓ Appreciate the value of being genuine, trusting, and confident.
- ✓ Gain satisfaction from visualizing short- and long-term goals.
- ✓ Be committed to setting personal priorities and be able to make rational trade-offs.

Liking yourself may be one of the most important things you'll have to do before you can become a high achiever. When you like yourself, you have self-confidence and you set goals for yourself that give purpose and direction in life.

And when you have self-confidence, your chances for success and high achievement are great. Liking yourself does not mean that you feel superior to others. Liking yourself means you have a positive self-image.

DO YOU HAVE A POSITIVE SELF-IMAGE?

When you have a positive self-image, it means that you feel confident about your abilities and feelings. In contrast, when you have a negative self-image, it means that you don't think much of yourself. Having a positive self-image can make the difference between success and failure. According to a famous doctor who made a detailed study of the self-image, you act like the person you conceive yourself to be.

Let us take a look at some examples. Al believed that he was slow in math. Sure enough, his report card usually had very low grades in math. Joyce believed that she was quiet and shy. Because she felt this way, she rarely had a date. Linda believed that she was a good mechanic. As a result of this belief, Linda studied engines and could often repair her own car. Pedro believed that he had leadership abilities. He ran for office in his club and served as a group leader in his church.

From the above examples, you may conclude that both Al and Joyce have negative self-images that prevent them from being successful. Although Al may never get A's in math, he could do much better with a positive self-image. Joyce may never win a public speaking contest, but with a positive self-image she could have more dates.

You may also conclude that Linda and Pedro have positive self-images because they are experiencing some success. Of course, Linda may not know how to fix her car every time something goes wrong with it, but her positive self-image will allow her to be successful most of the time. Pedro may lose some elections in the future, but his positive self-image will enable him to keep trying.

HOW TO DEVELOP A POSITIVE SELF-IMAGE

Here are six specific things you can do to attain a positive self-image: (1) accept yourself, (2) recognize your strengths and weaknesses, (3) overcome your fears, (4) engage in positive self-talk, (5) maintain good physical health, and (6) manage stress.

1. Accept Yourself

If you want to have a positive self-image, start by accepting yourself just as you are, here and now. If you want to become a better person, accept yourself first. Then you can change.

Some people never accept themselves and are constantly trying to change their personalities. They overlook the importance of self-acceptance. Trying to change without first accepting yourself is like trying to climb out of quicksand. The harder you try, the more impossible it becomes.

2. Recognize Your Strengths and Weaknesses

Self-accepting individuals know their strong points and weak points. Strong points are called personal strengths, and weak points are called personal weaknesses. Everyone has both personal strengths and weaknesses.

In the spaces in the next column, write a few of your personal strengths and weaknesses.

Illustration 7-1
Linda's success in construction leads to a positive self-image.

PERSONAL STRENGTHS

At School:
_____
_____
_____

At Work:
_____
_____
_____

PERSONAL WEAKNESSES

At School:
_____
_____
_____

At Work:
_____
_____
_____

If you are like most people, your list of weaknesses is longer than your list of strengths. Your list of weaknesses was also probably easier to write. Most people can recognize their weaknesses much more easily than they can recognize their strengths.

What to Do with Weaknesses. Self-accepting people recognize their weaknesses but do not dwell on them. Successful people maintain their composure in spite of their weaknesses. This means that they do not "go to pieces" over a mistake.

For example, in a game situation a player who makes a mistake and worries about it tends to make more mistakes. Being 100 percent ready for the next play means full concentration. Worrying about a mistake on a previous play hurts concentration. A player cannot be fully ready for the next play by dwelling on previous mistakes. Coaches want players who can shake off mistakes and keep going.

What to Do with Strengths. Successful people know their strong points and take advantage of them. This means that they put their personal strengths to work for themselves and others. They do not let their weaknesses hurt them.

For example, let us look at Herb, the assistant night manager of the Lucky Strike Bowling Alley. Herb is quite proud of his job because he worked hard to get it. Before he was promoted to his present position, Herb did just about every kind of job at Lucky Strike. It did not take him long to learn that he was not good at working with the automatic pinsetters (a weak point). But he enjoyed working at the desk and dealing with customers (a strong point).

One day the manager told Herb to repair the pinsetter on lane 12. Herb dreaded this task because he could not fix mechanical things easily. So, Herb said, "I can do it, but Sandy can fix it in about half the time it will take me to do it." This was hard for Herb to say, but he knew that he could show his worth to the manager in other ways. Because Herb could not fix mechanical things easily did not mean he was a failure at Lucky Strike. Herb knew that he could do the work at the front desk better than any of his co-workers. So he excelled at what he could do well. He did not let his weaknesses hurt him in his overall performance on the job.

3. Overcome Your Fears

No one is born confident. And no one is born with fear. Both being confident and being afraid are characteristics that are learned. The list of fears people have is endless. Here are some examples of fears that keep people from being successful:

◆ Fear of what others think or say
◆ Fear of losing a job
◆ Fear of failure in school
◆ Fear of relationships with others
◆ Fear of competition
◆ Fear of investing time and money

The truth is that 99 percent of all things people fear or worry about never happen. If you

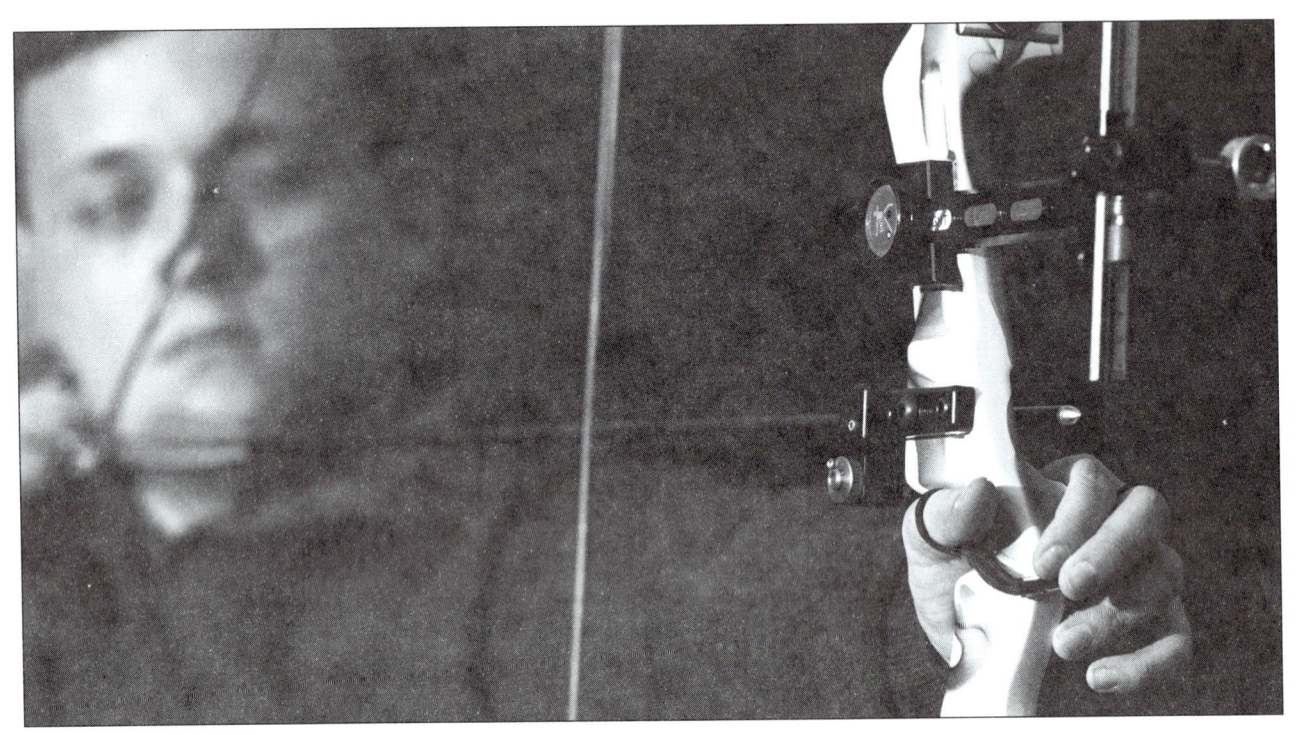

Illustration 7-2
A good player must be able to shake off mistakes and concentrate on the next play.

could redirect all the energy wasted on worrying into ways of taking advantage of strong points, you could be successful beyond all dreams. Yet, the problem is there: People do have fears. And to dismiss these fears with the old saying "It's all in your imagination" doesn't work. Fear is fear, whether it is real or imagined. This powerful force destroys confidence and leads to failure.[1]

Recognize That Fear Exists. In learning to be more confident, the first step is to recognize that fear exists. You must know what your fear is before you can do anything to overcome it.

Take Action to Eliminate Fear. When you know what your fear is and you do nothing about it, the fear grows and grows. Taking action to eliminate fear means more than simply "hoping for the best." It means actually doing something.

A good example of people experiencing fear frequently occurs in social relationships. At this very moment, someone is planning to ask another person to go on a date. We can increase the fear factor by about 100 if the person asking has never asked this particular person out. When you finally take action by speaking with the person, fear vanishes.

The case of Sara is a different example. Sara is a salesperson who goes from door to door selling cosmetics. For the last two months, sales have been down. Yesterday her supervisor called her into the office for the third time this month. Her supervisor laid it on the line and said, "Get those sales up or you may lose your job." Sara is worried about her appearance, her sales presentation, her bookkeeping, and the possibility of losing her job. She recognizes all these fears, but her action is limited because she is only "hoping for the best." What action should Sara take?

When people feel tense or anxious, they usually act in one of several ways. In Sara's case, she might get rid of her fears by talking to her supervisor, developing a plan to change her behavior, or finding a job other than sales.

---

[1]. For a more detailed examination of overcoming fear, see David J. Schwartz, The Magic of Thinking Big (Englewood Cliffs, NJ: Prentice-Hall, 1990). Parts of this section are inspired by the writings of Dr. Schwartz.

Failure to take action will probably result in stress. The ways to reduce stress are presented on page 198.

4. Engage in Positive Self-Talk

Everyone talks to himself or herself. On any particular day we probably talk to ourselves as much or more than we talk to other people. We don't talk out loud, yet we do have self-conversations.

Our awareness of this self-talk is heightened when we criticize ourselves, and most of us are very good at self-criticism. Positive self-talk is a way to stop the criticism. Generally we don't like to be around people who are negative and criticize a lot. When we are negative with ourselves, it hurts our self-image.

To avoid or minimize self-criticism, we can change negative self-talk to positive self-talk. Here are six starters:

Illustration 7-3
Sara the worrywart.

From negative Self-Talk

- I shouldn't have done . . .
- Why did I do . . . ?
- I can't . . .
- I hate . . .
- I really messed up . . .
- Why do people make me feel . . . ?

To POSITIVE Self-Talk

- Next time I will . . .
- It's not like me to do that . . .
- Maybe I can't do that, but this is what I can do . . .
- That's not always true . . .
- OK, so what? What's the worst possible thing that can happen?
- Nobody makes me feel a certain way. I choose how I feel, and I choose to feel good!

Positive self-talk can help you change your attitude toward a person, a project, or a problem. Use positive self-talk to change any negative or stressful situation. If you talk to yourself according to the suggestions given above, you can resolve difficult situations now. Why carry things around with you that hurt your self-image?

5. Maintain Good Physical Health

Good physical health is important to a good self-image. It is not easy to like ourselves if we are overweight or underweight, or poisoning our bodies with tobacco, alcohol, or other drugs.

The remarkable thing about good physical health is that it is so visible. The old saying about "bright eyes and a bushy tail" still rings true. People who have good physical health look good, have lots of energy, and are fun to be with.

Many businesses and organizations recognize the importance of good physical health. Employees are encouraged to exercise and eat properly. To demonstrate the value of healthy employees, some companies:

1. Provide exercise facilities for workouts before work, during the lunch period, and after work.
2. Participate in corporate track and other sporting events at the local, regional, or national levels.
3. Sponsor athletic events for charity.

4. Offer nutrition counseling.
5. Restrict smoking to specific areas outside of buildings.

In addition, company health insurance plans will generally treat alcohol and drug addiction as a medical problem. This means that individual counseling and rehabilitation costs are covered by insurance in much the same way as illness and surgery expenses. The value of good health is clearly recognized in such business practices.

6. Manage Stress

Exercise and diet are two good ways to maintain your health. But regular physical activity and proper eating habits won't guarantee a clean bill of health. Some jogging enthusiasts and health-food advocates have their share of illnesses. What causes some illness is the manner in which people approach their activities and eating habits.

Doctors who study chronic illnesses believe that as many as 70 percent of these illnesses are stress-related. This means that such things as sleeping problems, peptic ulcers, and even migraine headaches are related to stress. Indigestion is another way our bodies respond to the everyday stresses of life. Stomach-aches are often a physical symptom of prolonged or excessive stress.

Derek's sleeping problems are an example of a stress-related problem. Derek always has trouble falling asleep the night before an exam. His sleeping problem is an indication of his concern about doing well on the exam. His inability to sleep shows that emotions and the everyday stresses of his life do influence what happens to his health.

Stress symptoms also occur at work. Joan's anxiety over her performance appraisals is a good example. After she received a low rating and was passed over for a promotion, Joan began to lose effectiveness in her job. She com-

Illustration 7-4
Being physically fit is important for managing stress.

plained of being tired all the time, and the sparkle in her eye was gone. Joan's reaction to her performance appraisal demonstrates the mental impact of stress.

Both Derek and Joan can learn to manage the stresses in their lives. An effective way to overcome stress is to avoid stress-producing situations. But it is not always possible to avoid situations that provoke stress. Derek can't avoid exams if he plans to graduate. And Joan can't avoid performance appraisals if she wants to stay in her job. What Derek and Joan can do is to use stress in a positive way. Instead of merely coping with stress, they can actively manage what happens in their everyday lives. Both of them have the power to overcome stress by taking charge of those things that can be changed.

For example, if Derek has a habit of cramming the night before exams, he can start a regular study program. This will give him more time to learn. He may even learn more with the additional time. If Joan can never find her weekly reports, she can put an end to her anxiety by cleaning up her work area. Such tensions can be managed positively. The important thing to remember is that stress can be positive when it energizes you instead of slowing you down. If you learn to avoid stressful situations or manage those that can't be avoided, you will have more energy for creative projects and recreational activities.

CHARACTERISTICS OF HIGH ACHIEVERS

High achievers tend to be liked by other people. If people like you, it is because you possess certain qualities that make you likable. Some important qualities are given below. Try to add to this list of qualities in the spaces provided.
- Being a good sport
- Being easy to talk with
- Having a good sense of humor
- Dressing nicely
- _____
- _____
- _____

There are many other valuable qualities that make a person likable. The two qualities most characteristic of high achievers are (1) being genuine and (2) being trustworthy.

Be a Genuine Person

Being genuine means being yourself. Genuine people do not put up false fronts to try to look good. Genuine people do not put on an act. Genuine people are comfortable with themselves.

The value of being genuine can be illustrated by looking at what makes a successful life insurance salesperson. In order to succeed in selling life insurance, the salesperson must possess many important qualities. But, first of all, the salesperson must be genuine because this particular job usually requires more than one contact with a prospective customer. If the prospective customer does not see this salesperson as a genuine human being during the first meeting, chances are that the salesperson will not succeed in making a sale.

Several studies have already been made by executives in the insurance business that indicate that most people buy insurance because they like the salesperson. The name of the insurance company represented by the salesperson is usually not the main reason why people buy insurance.

One large insurance company wanted to increase its sales. It conducted an expensive and time-consuming study to find out if sales might be related to the type of salesperson. The executives of this company wondered, for example, if the pushy, hard-sell type is more successful than the soft-sell type. Or does the good-looking, outgoing person produce more sales than the average-looking, quiet person? To find the answers to these questions, a test was given to all the top insurance salespersons of the company. The results of this study showed that:
1. The fast-talking, hard-hitting person sells about the same amount of insurance as the slow-talking, easygoing person.
2. The average-looking person sells just as much insurance as the good-looking person.

In other words, no particular type of salesperson sold more insurance than other types of salespersons. The study concluded that only one single factor is related to sales: genuineness. The high-achieving salespersons of this company were genuine because they reflected their own personalities and knew how to use their own abilities. These particular salespersons did not pretend to be someone else.

The horizontal line in Illustration 7-5 and the vertical line in Illustration 7-6 show parts of the test that were given to the insurance salespersons. Both lines are divided into four equal parts. Read the brief descriptions given in these illustrations.

Now try this test by putting an *X* in one of the four sections of the horizontal line and the vertical line. For example, if you believe that you are very assertive, place an *X* in the farthest section to the right of the horizontal line in Illustration 7-5. And if you believe that you are very informal, place an *X* in the lowest section of the vertical line in Illustration 7-6.

Illustration 7-7 shows how Laura plotted her *X*'s on the horizontal line and the vertical line. Her *X*'s have been transferred to the personality grid in Illustration 7-8. After you have plotted your *X*'s on the lines in Illustrations 7-5 and 7-6, transfer them to the grid in Illustration 7-8. Remember that the insurance company study showed that each type of person sells about the same amount of insurance. This means that each of the styles on the grid can be successful.

LOW RESPONSIVENESS

Very Formal
Formal

Independent of others; tends to be cool, formal, controlled, and cautious with feelings.

Informal
Very Informal

Involved with others; tends to be casual, fun loving, and open with feelings.

HIGH RESPONSIVENESS

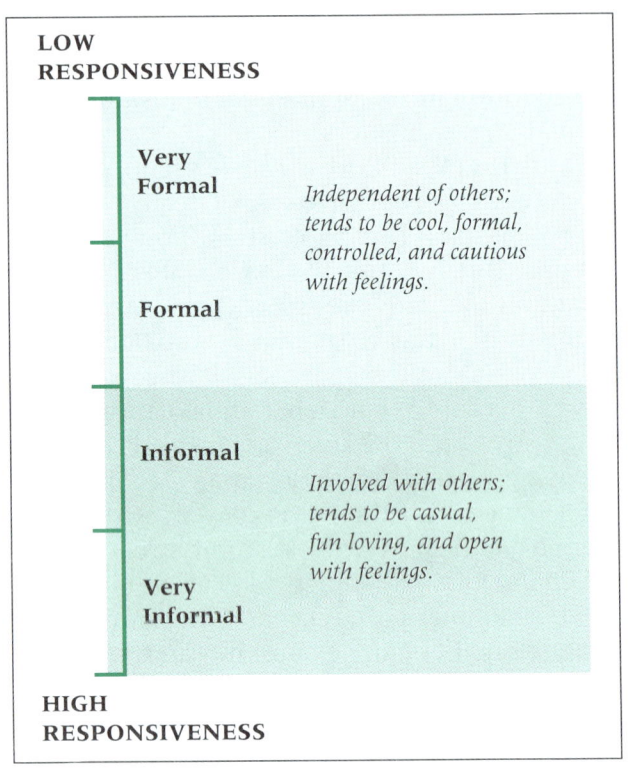

Illustration 7-6
Vertical line showing degree of responsiveness.

Very Easygoing | Easygoing | Assertive | Very Assertive

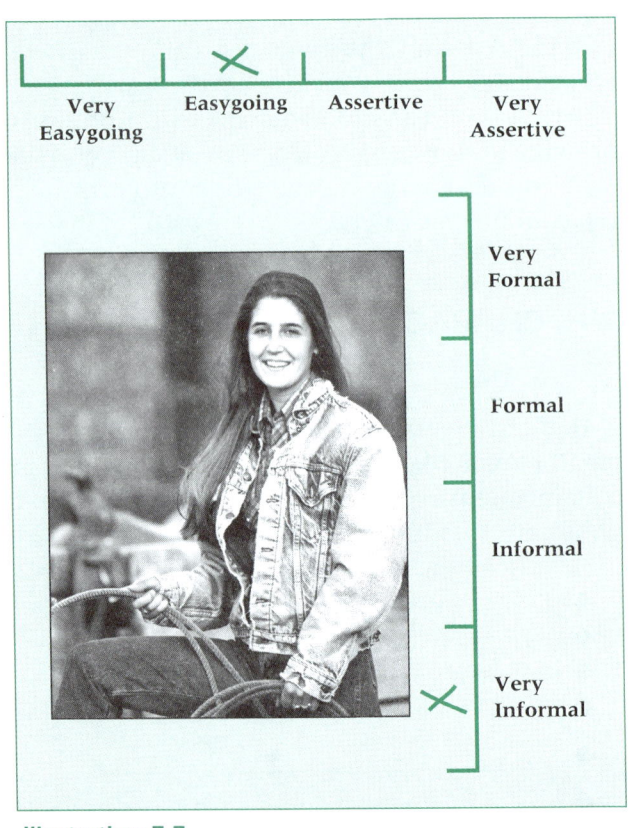

Very Formal
Formal
Informal
Very Informal

Illustration 7-7
Laura thinks of herself as easygoing and very informal. Her X's on the profile are shown above.

Very Easygoing	Easygoing	Assertive	Very Assertive
Likes to be unimposing with others. Asks questions and listens, but may not talk unless there is a specific reason to do so.		*Likes to know what is going on and takes action to find out. Talks a lot with others—even when it may not be wise to do so.*	

Illustration 7-5
Horizontal line showing degree of assertiveness.

LEGEND

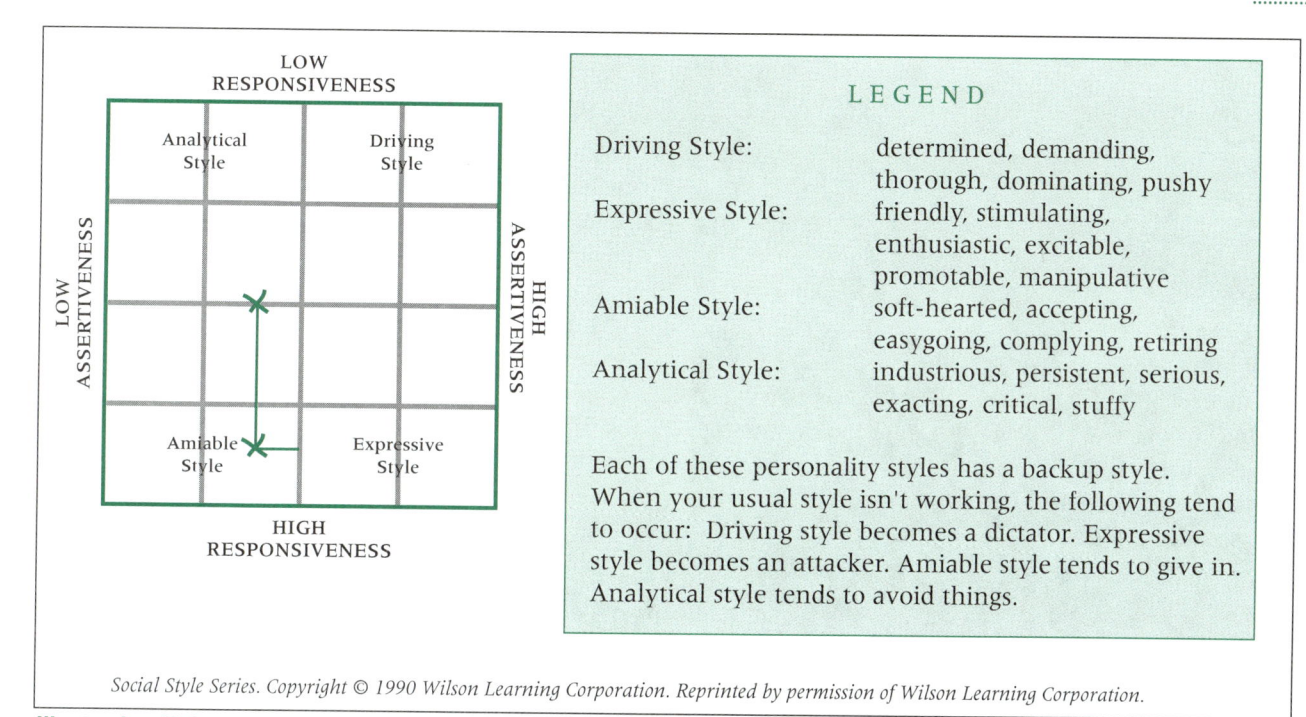

Driving Style:	determined, demanding, thorough, dominating, pushy
Expressive Style:	friendly, stimulating, enthusiastic, excitable, promotable, manipulative
Amiable Style:	soft-hearted, accepting, easygoing, complying, retiring
Analytical Style:	industrious, persistent, serious, exacting, critical, stuffy

Each of these personality styles has a backup style. When your usual style isn't working, the following tend to occur: Driving style becomes a dictator. Expressive style becomes an attacker. Amiable style tends to give in. Analytical style tends to avoid things.

Social Style Series. Copyright © 1990 Wilson Learning Corporation. Reprinted by permission of Wilson Learning Corporation.

Illustration 7-8
Personality grid.

Be a Trustworthy Person

When you are trustworthy, it means that others will take risks with you because they have confidence in your abilities. The two key terms to understand here are risk and confidence.

Taking a risk means taking a chance. The greater the risk of anything, the more trust is involved. For example, how often do you count your change when you buy something? Well, it probably depends on the amount of change you should receive. Say you buy a soft drink and pay for it with a one-dollar bill. Since your change will be small, you probably do not count it very closely. But suppose you pay for the soft drink with a ten-dollar bill. Chances are that you will count your change more carefully than you would when only one dollar is involved. You do this because your risk of loss is greater when ten dollars is involved.

The other part of being trustworthy is related to confidence. Assume for a moment that you are at a basketball game. The score is tied 60 to 60, and only five seconds remain to end the game. The team you are rooting for gets the ball and quickly calls "time out." Which player will the coach pick to take the last shot? Naturally the coach will choose the best player. The coach chooses this player because the coach has confidence in this player's ability to get the job done.

How to Build Trusting Relationships

The key to building trusting relationships with others is to be trustworthy yourself. When others take risks with you, you must prove that their risks are worth taking. And when others show confidence in you, you must justify their confidence by being reliable.

One way to establish a trusting relationship with someone is to risk being open about yourself. Consider the case of Maria, who met Ella for the first time. This is what Maria had to say.

"I started to work at Macy's today. I went on morning break and then to lunch with Ella. She is not my age but we have a lot in common. At the morning break we talked about her. At lunch we talked about me. I was surprised that I said so much about myself. I told her some things that I have never told anyone before, but I am glad I did."

Illustration 7-9
Maria builds trusting relationaships by taking a risk in telling Ella many things about herself.

Maria risked telling Ella many things about herself. The risk could involve being rejected, being ridiculed, or being taken advantage of by Ella. But the risk Maria took was worth it because Ella accepted her. Thus, the first step toward a trusting relationship between these two persons has taken place.

A trusting relationship with someone can also develop when you show that you can be relied on to get things done. For example, Irving, who was Manuel's supervisor at work, had this to say:

"Manuel surely made our store look good last week. While I was gone, one of our best customers came into the store and was very angry. This fellow wanted to know why we hadn't delivered the goods he ordered and demanded to see me. Manuel found this customer's two-week-old order on my desk. It was marked 'not in stock'. Manuel got right on the phone, called one of our competitors, and filled the order. I am sure Manuel saved this account by his quick action. It is a good feeling to know you can rely on your employees."

Manuel knew that his supervisor had confidence in his ability. Manuel justified this confidence by getting the job done in Irving's absence.

CHECK YOUR UNDERSTANDING

To be sure you are reading and learning the key points, fill in the blanks with the missing word or group of words.

1. List two of six ways to develop a positive self-image.

_____
_____
_____

2. Two universal qualities of high achievers are:

_____
_____
_____

3. The key to building trustworthy relationships is to

_____
_____
_____
_____
_____ .

DO YOU SET GOALS IN LIFE?

High achievers have career goals. A goal is something you plan to achieve. It gives you purpose and direction in life. An example of a goal at school could be to earn good grades, hold elected office, or earn a letter on a varsity team. At work, a goal might be to get high efficiency ratings from your supervisor.

SHORT-TERM AND LONG-TERM GOALS

Organizations classify goals as short-term or long-term. A short-term goal could be set for a day, a week, or a month. Any objective that can be accomplished in less than a year's time is called a short-term goal. An example of a short-term goal could be to get an A grade in this course. Another example could be to have a full-time summer job that leads to a career.

Long-term goals take more time to achieve than short-term goals. Any objective that takes more than a year's time to accomplish is a long-term goal. An example of a long-term goal could be to graduate from a community college. Another example could be to become an assistant store manager in five years.

Short- and long-term goals will help you get ahead in life. You can do more and better things when you set goals. No company ever made a profit without goals. Organizations set goals for 5, 10, and even 15 years ahead. Some Asian companies have set goals 100 years in advance. Each year and each month organizations set short-term goals to help reach long-term goals. Organizations do not leave the future to chance. Do you?

> *The game of life is not so much in holding a good hand as in playing a poor hand well.*
>
> - H. T. Leslie

GOAL-SETTING GUIDELINES

As you plan both types of goals, consider the guidelines given below.

1. Who owns the goal? Does the goal belong to you or to someone else? If you set the goal yourself, this means it is yours. Others may give or sell you a goal, but it won't work unless you believe in the goal. When you believe in a goal, you can call the goal your own. The goals you own have a good chance of being accomplished.

2. Is the goal under your control? A goal is under your control if the result depends on your own actions. You are less likely to achieve a goal if you have to depend unnecessarily on somebody's action to accomplish it. Look at the following examples:

Goals Dependent on Yourself
- I will get to work on time by getting myself up at 7:00 A.M.
- On Monday I will ask Cecilia to the dance on Friday night.

A Goal Dependent on Others
- I will let Cecilia know that I want to date her by having Alex tell her so.

Illustration 7-10
Short-term and long-term goals.

3. Is the goal measurable? How do you know when you reach a goal? If a goal is stated in specific terms, you will know. The more precisely a goal is stated, the easier it is to know when you reach it. Look at the following examples:

Unmeasurable Goals

- I will devote more time to studying.
- I will get involved in activities at school.

Measurable Goals

- I will devote five hours each week to studying by using study periods at school strictly for studying.
- I will attend at least three of the home basketball games.
- I will join a club or organization that does at least two activities at school each month.

4. Does the goal have a time limit? Without a specific time limit, a goal is meaningless. In the absence of such a limit, it would be possible to put off achieving the goal. Time limits provide the target date.

No Time Limit

- I will save $1,000.
- I will visit my grandmother.

Time Limit

- I will save $1,000 over a period of the next 12 months.
- I will visit my grandmother on her birthday this year.

Using the table below, try writing two goals that meet the goal-setting guidelines.

SETTING PRIORITIES

You make choices about what to do every day. Some things you must do today. Other things you could do today, tomorrow, or the next day. The process of deciding which things to do today, tomorrow, next week, next month, and so on is called setting priorities.

Everyone has written or unwritten lists of things to do. For example, Sam might have the following items on a list of things to do:

- Studying schoolwork
- Working part-time
- Making car payments
- Going out with friends
- Visiting relatives

A list of things to do becomes a list of priorities when numbers are assigned to the items on the list. Below is Sam's list of priorities:

1. Working part-time
2. Making car payments
3. Going out with friends
4. Studying schoolwork
5. Visiting relatives

Note that "studying schoolwork" doesn't rank very high on Sam's list of priorities. His job, car, and friends are more important to him than schoolwork. It is not surprising that at the end of the term Sam's report card showed low grades.

GOAL STATEMENT	Goal-Setting Guidelines			
	Do you own the goal?	Is it under your control?	Is it measurable?	Is there a time limit?

Illustration 7-11
Studying is now Sam's top priority.

CHANGING PRIORITIES

Sometimes it becomes necessary to change priorities. Let us go back to Sam's case and see why he had to change his priorities. Sam's parents were very displeased with his low grades. They told him that if his grades didn't improve during the next term, he would have to quit working. That would mean giving up his car. Sam therefore changed his priorities. Studying is now Sam's top priority. By studying more, Sam will improve his grades. Then he can keep his job and his car and still go out with friends.

MAKING TRADE-OFFS

The process of giving up some things in return for other things is called making trade-offs. In order to reach a goal, making trade-offs is often necessary. In Sam's case, for example, he must decrease the amount of time for some things in order to increase his study time—his present goal.

Sam's Goal
◆ To increase study time by . . .

Sam's Alternatives
1. Cutting out TV on weekdays
2. Staying home on weeknights
3. Going to school early to study
4. Using study time given in class for studying

Sam will achieve his goal by taking action on one or more alternatives. Since Sam wants to keep his car, wants to keep his job, and wants to earn good grades, he traded off some time for watching TV and some time for going out with friends. In return, Sam had more time for studying.

People in business make trade-offs, too. Successful people in business consider as many alternatives as possible. By doing so, they are ready to make wise decisions and can avoid unwise trade-offs.

> *One who learns but does not think is lost. One who thinks but does not learn is in great danger.*
>
> - Confucius

NET WORKING

Join us on the Internet. Check out our Human Relations for Career Success Home Page.

Try some of our special Internet Activities for Chapter 7. Your instructor will give you instructions on which activities would be good for you to complete.

Connect with us at:

http://success.swpco.com

CHAPTER 7 ◆ BECOMING A HIGH ACHIEVER **207**

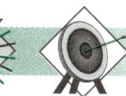

Activity 7-1
RECOGNIZING STRENGTHS

Assume that you are very close to being hired for a job. This job is especially important because it is the one job you have been hoping would be offered to you.

The only thing standing between you and this job is a letter of recommendation. You have asked a friend to write this letter. Write the letter to the prospective employer that you would like your friend to write.

Hint: Try using a five-paragraph approach. In paragraph one indicate why your are writing to the employer. In paragraph two comment on the person's (your) ability to work with customers (refer to Chapter 2, Customer Focus). Next write about the person's ability to get along well with others (refer to Chapter 3, Teamwork). In the fourth paragraph write about the person's communications skills, say, listening or giving feedback. Conclude with an invitation to call you to talk in more detail about the person and his or her qualifications.

Dear Prospective Employer:

_____
_____
_____
_____
_____
_____
_____
_____
_____
_____
_____
_____
_____
_____
_____
_____
_____
_____
_____

Activity 7-1, continued

Activity 7-2
ELIMINATING FEAR

Remember how Sara's fears (see page 196) made her a mental wreck on the job? Here is another story, about Rex, whose fears get in the way of his performance on the job. Read the following story and then answer the questions. Be prepared to discuss your answers in class.

Rex is a part-time sacker at the local grocery store. Rex believes that he is a quiet and shy person. As a result of his belief, Rex rarely talks to the customers or his boss. He is afraid of making mistakes on the job. His boss wonders why Rex spends so much time looking over his shoulder or just fidgeting.

1. Does Rex like himself? Explain your answer.

2. What does Rex need to accept about himself?

3. Is being quiet and shy a weakness of Rex's?

4. What are some strong points about being quiet and shy?

Activity 7-2, continued

5. How can Rex build confidence in himself?

6. What action can Rex take to eliminate his fears?

Activity 7-3
THE STRESS SCALE

Characteristics of Stress-Prone Individuals

Answer these three questions with a Yes or No:

_____ 1. Do you have a habit of doing two or three projects at the same time?

_____ 2. Do you have a tendency to count things as you work?

_____ 3. Are you critical of people who are always late for appointments?

The people who develop stress tests believe that frequent or prolonged stress directly relates to your predicted illness level. It is believed that you can control stress-related illnesses with regular exercise, recreational activities, and a moderate diet.

If you answered yes to all three questions, you may have some of the characteristics of a stress-prone individual. Although few of us live without stress, prolonged or excessive stress can have serious physical and mental consequences.

Strategies for Managing Stress

In the left-hand column, list the behaviors you have observed in yourself or in others that may be stress related. Use the right-hand column to list at least two actions that could help manage the stress.

Stress-Related Behaviors

1. _____

2. _____

3. _____

4. _____

5. _____

Strategies for Managing Stress

1. a. _____
   b. _____

2. a. _____
   b. _____

3. a. _____
   b. _____

4. a. _____
   b. _____

5. a. _____
   b. _____

Activity 7-4
TRUST WALK

Members of the class should form pairs. One person will be the guide for the trust walk; the other will be blindfolded. The guide takes the hand or arm of the blindfolded partner through an obstacle course in the room. Points are earned by making it around the barriers. As a group, you decide on the barriers and the points. Switch roles after one partner is led through the course.

An alternative for this activity is to omit the points and simply walk around the building.

After the trust walk, answer the following questions in the spaces provided.

1. Did you trust your guide near the end of the walk? Explain your answer.

2. Did you trust your guide at first? Explain your answer.

3. How did it feel to depend on someone?

4. How did it feel to have someone depend on you?

5. What did you learn about your guide when you were led around?

6. What did you learn about your blindfolded partner as you led this person around?

CHAPTER 7 ◆ BECOMING A HIGH ACHIEVER **215**

Activity 7-5
TAKING RISKS

Trust develops when you risk being open about yourself with others.

Part 1
Try completing the following sentences as openly and honestly as you can. You may choose not to complete some sentences, for that is your right.

1. I am most comfortable when I
   _____
   _____
   _____

2. I worry most about
   _____
   _____
   _____
   _____

3. I like to spend my free time on
   _____
   _____
   _____
   _____

4. I like/don't like certain people because
   _____
   _____
   _____
   _____
   _____

5. I believe/don't believe in something I am told because
   _____
   _____
   _____
   _____
   _____

6. I agree/don't agree with my friends when they say
   _____
   _____
   _____
   _____

7. Even though my friends don't agree, I like to
   _____
   _____
   _____
   _____

8. I like/don't like people who
   _____
   _____
   _____

Activity 7-5, continued

9. I admire others who _____

10. I get angry with others when they _____

Part 2
Now go back over your statements. Which of these beliefs and feelings are you willing to tell others? Which can you tell a close friend, the people you work with, your supervisor, or your parents? Which statements are you unwilling to reveal even to a close friend? Read the following questions and think about your answers:

1. Why is it considered risky to reveal personal beliefs? _____

2. Do you know people who ridicule others when these others share their personal beliefs? _____

3. How can you take risks in revealing yourself to others without fearing rejection or ridicule by them? _____

4. Which of the statements in Part 1 would you now risk revealing to a close friend? _____

5. Does your own trust increase when you risk telling others about yourself? _____

Share your answer to Question 3 in class. What kinds of help have others in the class suggested?

Activity 7-6
LIFE LINES

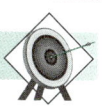

Follow these directions:

1. In the space below, draw a horizontal line. Let the line represent your past, present, and future.

2. Place an X on the line to show where you are today.

3. Place a Y on the line to represent where you expect to be five years from now.

4. On the bottom of this page, write a description of yourself as you see yourself five years from now.

5. Write a long-term goal for yourself.

6. Write three short-term goals that will help you reach the long-term goal you just wrote. Be sure your goals are measurable.

How I see myself five years from now:

___
___
___
___
___

A personal long-term goal:

___
___
___
___
___

Three short-term goals:

___
___
___
___
___

Activity 7-7
PRIORITIES AND TRADE-OFFS

Based on what you have learned in this chapter, answer the following questions.

1. What are priorities?

2. List your priorities for this week.

3. Write three examples of trade-offs that you or someone you know chose to make.

4. How do trade-offs differ from quitting?

Activity 7-8
GOLD IN GOALS

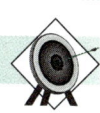

This activity is titled Gold in Goals because of the value of goals and in the reward you will receive when you reach your goals.

Part 1
Answer the questions below. Then use these answers to help you complete Part 2.

How do you know who owns a goal?
_____
_____
_____
_____

A goal is under your control if . . .
_____
_____
_____
_____
_____

A measurable goal is stated in . . .
_____
_____
_____
_____
_____

A goal without a time limit is . . .
_____
_____
_____
_____
_____

Part 2
The four items in the first column are criteria for writing goals. Use the criteria to write a personal goal in each of the following categories.

Schoolwork
_____
_____
_____
_____
_____

Career
_____
_____
_____
_____
_____

Personal Finance
_____
_____
_____
_____
_____

Community Service
_____
_____
_____
_____
_____

Index

A

Absolute statements, 120, 125
Acceptance, 56-59
   honesty and, 95
   of praise, 70-71
   self-image and, 194
   strengths/weaknesses and self-, 195
Advancement, 69
Advertising, word-of-mouth, 28-29
Advice, 158
   with child care, 8
   management styles and, 99
Affirmative action, 6-8
Age. *See* Older people, discrimination against
Age Discrimination in Employment Act, 7
Alcohol, 197, 198
Allness, 120-122
Alternatives, direct vs. indirect, 68
Americans with Disabilities Act, 7
Amiable personality, 201
Analytical personality, 201
Appearance
   acceptance and, 58-59
   clothing and, 59
   customers and, 23-24
Arab countries, 58
Asian culture, 57, 58, 203
Assertiveness, 200, 201
Assumptions, 58
Athletic events, 197
Attacker style, 201
Attendance, health and, 8
Attention, 25-27
   to employees (from supervisors), 4-5
   from employees (to customers), 25-27
Attitudes
   communication and, 118
   toward customers, 31-32
   employee health and, 8
   "good," 59
Australia, 57
Authoritarian managers, 99
Authority, 130, 131-132
   human rights and, 170

B

Behavior
   brain dominance theory and, 164
   expectations for, 156-157, 160
   inner-directed, 156, 159-161
   other- and inner-directed, 156, 159
   other-directed, 156, 157, 158
   personal beliefs and, 159-161, 164-171
   prescriptions for, 158, 160
   separating person from, 67-68
   trial-and-error method for, 158-159, 160
Benefit plans
   contract and, 60
   equal employment opportunity and, 7
   in 1950s, 6
Brain dominance theory, 164
Brazil, 58
Business
   growth of, 91, 96, 171
   profit and, 90-91
Business reputation, 91, 103
   customer service and, 28-29
   values and, 171
   word-of-mouth advertising and, 28-29
Business strategy, 8

C

Change
   conflict and, 65-68
   employment security and, 93
   in priorities, 205
Channel selection, 118, 119
Charity, 91, 197
Child care, 8. *See also* Day care
Children, parental leave for, 7, 8
Civil Rights Act (1964), 7
Clients, 2
Clothing
   assumptions based on, 58, 59
   authoritarian managers and, 99
   dress code for, 23
   of other cultures, 56, 57
Coaches (employers as), 97-98
Color (discrimination based on), 7
Commitment, 6, 24
Communication
   barriers to, 119-125
   defined, 118-119
   electronic, 136-138
   formal organization for official, 130-132
   grapevine for, 132-134, 135, 136
   informal organization for unofficial, 130, 132-136
   interpersonal, 117-153
   interrupting and, 130
   listening in, 125, 126-130
   misuse of language in, 122-125
   non-face-to-face, 136-137
   nonverbal, 130, 136
   official vs. unofficial, 130-136
   rumors and, 134-136
   semantics and, 119-120
   training in, 117
Community
   other firms in, 103, 104
   reputation in, 91, 171. *See also* Business reputation
   service work in, 8. *See also* Charity
Competence, employee, 25, 94
Competition, fear of, 195
Competitive advantage, 8
Competitive prices, 171
Computers
   customer database on, 26
   electronic communication by, 136-138
Confidence, 200-201, 202. *See also* Self-confidence
Conflict, misunderstandings and, 119
Conflict management, 65-68
Consideration, 61-62
Continuous improvement, 101, 102-103
Contract, 60, 91-96
   unwritten, 92-96
Control, goals and, 203
Cooperation, 64
Corporate sporting events, 197
Counseling, 8, 198, 199
Co-workers
   acceptance by, 56
   attitudes toward, 59
   communication from, 132. *See also* Grapevine
   conflict with, 65-68
   consideration toward, 61-62
   cooperating with, 64
   customers and, 33
   embarrassing, 63
   getting along with, 62-71

relationships with, 2, 3, 9
territorial rights of, 61
tolerance and, 65-68
See also Teamwork
Creativity, 171
Criticism, 197
Cultures
accepting other, 57-58
conflict with other, 65
Customer expectations, 22-29
Customer focus, 19-54
Customer needs, 29-31
diverse, 8
Customer service, 20, 22-29
customer card file/database and, 26
vs. service organizations, 20
and word-of-mouth advertising, 28-29
Customers
angry or dissatisfied, 32-33
attitude toward, 31-32
card file of, 26-27
defined, 2, 29
different types of, 29-31
guidelines/steps for dealing with, 30-31, 32-33
honesty with, 95
importance of, 20
"moment of truth" with, 23, 27-29
quality and, 101
recognition of, 25
relationships with, 2, 9, 29, 171
remembering names of, 25
synonyms for, 2

D

Database, customer, 26
Day care, 7. *See also* Child care
Decision making, 6
EitherOr thinking in, 122
management styles and, 99-101
quality and, 102
shared, 6
trade-offs in, 206
types of, 103
values and, 168-169, 171
Delegation (of duties), 100, 103
Democratic managers, 99-100
Dependability, customers and, 24
Dictator style, 201
Diet, 8, 198
Disability/disabled
affirmative action and, 8
discrimination based on, 7
values and, 171
See also Handicapped people
Discrimination, 6
laws against, 7
in services, 22
sex, 7, 124
age, 6, 7
Diverse work force, 8
Downgrades, 7
Dress code, 23
Driving personality, 201
Drug testing, 8
Drug-Free Workplace Act, 8
Drugs, 197, 198. *See also* Substance abuse

E

E-mail, 136, 137-138
Education, in affirmative action, 8
Effectiveness, 87-115
EitherOr thinking, 121-122
Elder care, 8
Electronic communication, 136-138
Emotional confusion, 122, 123-124
Emotions
communication and, 118, 122, 123-125
listening and, 127-128, 130
stress and, 198
See also Feelings
Empathy, 125
Employee expectations, 92-94
Employee handbooks, 60, 63
Employee recognition, 6, 69, 92
Employee satisfaction, 69
Employees
appearance of, 23
attention from (to customers), 25
attention to (from supervisors), 4-5
commitment of, 6, 24
competence of, 25, 94
dependability of, 24
desirable traits of, 94-96
honesty of, 95
potential of, 6
responsiveness of, 24-25
Western Electric experiment and, 5
Employers, 88-91
as coaches and mentors, 97-98
expectations of, 92, 94-96, 104
as human beings, 89-90
management styles of, 98-101
relationships with, 3, 4, 9, 87-104
success and, 90-91, 94, 96
typical day of, 103
Western Electric experiment and, 5
See also Managers; Supervisors
Employment contract, 60, 91-96
unwritten, 92-96
Employment discrimination, 6
equal employment opportunity and, 7
laws against, 7
Employment security, 93-94
Environment, respect for, 91
Environmental requirements (of employee), 92-93
Equal employment opportunity, 6-7
Equal Pay Act, 7
Equipment
appearance of, 23
responsibility for, 96
Ethnic harassment, 8
Exercise, 8, 197, 198
Expectations
behavior directed by, 156-157, 160
customer, 22-29
employee, 92-94
employer, 92, 94-96, 104
Expressive personality, 201
Eye contact, 58

F

Facilities
appearance of, 23
disabled people and, 8
Facts
listening and, 128-129, 130
quality and, 102
Failure (fear of), 195
Fairness, 91, 92, 171
Family and Medical Leave Act, 7
Family/work issues, 8
FAQ. *See* Frequently asked questions (FAQ)
Fear (overcoming), 195-197
Feedback, 97, 118, 119
verbal vs. nonverbal, 136
Feelings
communication and, 118
electronic communication and, 136
employee expectations and, 92
listening and, 129, 130
self-knowledge and, 163
See also Emotions
Financial records, 103

Firing. *See* Terminations
Flattery, 70, 71
Flexible workplace, 7, 8
Formal organization, 130-132
Formal personality, 200
Frequently asked questions (FAQ), 137-138

G

Gender, values and, 171
Genuineness, 199-200
"Global village," 57
Goals
 in affirmative action, 8
 guidelines for setting, 203-205
 measurable, 204
 organizational, 203
 personal, 193, 203-206
 priorities and, 205
 short-term vs. long-term, 203
 trade-offs and, 205-206
Goods, 20
 knowledge of, 31
 See also Product quality; Products
Goodwill, 22, 96
Government
 equal employment opportunity and, 7
 quality award from, 101
Grapevine, 132-134, 135, 136
Groups
 informal, 132
 small, 6

H

Handicapped people
 employment discrimination and, 6
 See also Disability/disabled
Harassment, 8
Hawthorne Effect, 4
Health
 physical and mental, 8
 self-image and, 197-198
Health insurance, 198
Hiring, 7
Holidays, 60
Home (working at), 8
Honesty, 162
 of business, 91
 of employees, 95
Human relations
 careers in, 2-4
 communication and, 118, 121, 122, 124, 125, 126
 customer card file/database and, 26
 defined, 2
 electronic communication and, 136
 history of, 4-8
 honesty and, 95
 importance of, 4-5
 labeling and, 122
 people knowledge as, 9
 self-knowledge and, 162
 success through, 8-9
 understanding, 1-18
 words and, 124
Human relations movement, 4-8
Human rights, 170-171

I

Illness
 family, 7, 8
 sick leave for, 63
 stress-related, 198
Immigrants, 57
Industriousness, 96
Informal organization, 130, 132-136
Informal personality, 200, 201
Information, 97
 rumors and, 136
 about yourself, 161-162
 See also Communication; Facts
Injuries, 8
Inner-directed behavior, 156, 159-161
Innovation, 171
Insurance, health, 198
Integrity, 171
Internet, 136, 137
Interpersonal communication, 117-153
Interpersonal requirements (of employee), 92, 93
Israel, 57

J

Japanese culture, 57, 58
Job(s)
 fear of losing, 195
 "good," 55
 titles of, 123-124
Job skills
 employment security and, 93
 learning future, 94
 technical, 9
Johari Window, 161-162, 163
Justice, 168-171

K

Knowledge
 of goods and services, 31
 of people, 9
 of self, 162-163
 technical, 9

L

Labeling, 122-123, 125
Labor unions, 60, 61
Laissez-faire management style, 100-101
LAN. *See* Local area network (LAN)
Language
 misuse of, 122-125
 sexist, 124
 See also Communication; Words
Laws
 drug-testing, 8
 equal employment opportunity, 7
 human rights and, 170
Layoffs
 contract and, 60
 equal employment opportunity and, 7
Learning
 brain dominance theory of, 164
 of job skills, 93, 94
 about yourself, 161-162
Learning response, 65-66
Leave (of absence), 7, 8. *See also* Sick leave
Life-styles
 accepting other, 56-58
 healthy, 8
LIFO (Last In to work and First one Out), 64
Lines of authority, 130-132
Lines of communication, 132, 133. *See also* Communication
Listening, 125, 126-130
 facts and, 128-129, 130
 feelings and, 129, 130
 improving, 129-130
Local area network (LAN), 136
Long-term goals, 203
Loyalty, employee, 94
Luck, 161

M

Malcolm Baldrige National Quality Award, 101
Management, participative, 100
Management by objectives, 6
Management styles, 98-101
Managers
 authority and, 130, 131-132
 communication and, 118, 120, 129
 listening by, 129

organization chart and, 130
sexist language and, 124
values and, 171
See also Employers; Supervisors
Measurable goals, 204
Mental disability, 7
Mental health programs, 8
Mentors, 97-98
Merchandise, responsibility for, 96
Minorities
affirmative action and, 8
employment discrimination and, 6
"Moment of truth," 23, 27-29
Money, 69
fear of investing, 195
responsibility for, 95
See also Pay; Salary

N

Name calling, 122-123
National origin, 7
Negative self-image, 194
Negative self-talk, 197
Nigeria, 57
Nonverbal communication, 130, 136

O

Objectives, management by, 6
Occupational titles, 123-124
Older people, discrimination against, 6
Organization
formal, 130-132
informal, 130, 132-136
Organization chart, 130, 131, 132
Organizational activities, internal, 87
Organizational effectiveness, 87-115
Other-directed behavior, 156, 157, 158
inner- and, 156, 159
Oversimplification, 120-121
Ownership (of goals), 203

P

Part-time work, 8
Participative management, 100
Pay
contract and, 60
industriousness and, 96
See also Money; Salary
People, 2
competitive advantage through, 8
knowledge about, 9
processes vs., 101-102

words and, 119, 120, 125. *See also* Communication
See also Human relations; Relationship(s)
Performance appraisal, 198-199
Personal attention, 25-27, 33
Personal beliefs
behavior and, 159-161
values and, 164-171
Personal satisfaction, 69
Personal strengths/weaknesses, 194-195
Personality
assertive vs. easygoing, 200, 201
emotions and, 127-128
genuineness and, 200
grid for, 200, 201
informal vs. formal, 200
listening and, 127-128
self-image and, 194
styles of, 201
Personnel, 7, 23. *See also* Employees; Human relations
Phased retirement, 8
Physical disability, 7, 171. *See also* Handicapped people
Physical health
programs for, 8
self-image and, 197-198
Physical power, 169
Planning, 99-101
Policy
communication and, 132
customers and, 33
democratic managers and, 99
employee handbooks and, 60
See also Rules
Positive self-image, 193, 194-202. *See also* Self-image
Positive self-talk, 197
Positive words, 124, 125
Power, 169
Praise, accepting, 70-71
Prejudice, 8. *See also* Discrimination
Prescriptions (for behavior), 158, 160
Priorities, 205
Privileges
equal employment opportunity and, 7
flaunting, 71
industriousness and, 96
seniority system and, 61
Problem solving
EitherOr thinking in, 122
quality and, 102
small-group, 6
values and, 171
Processes, quality and, 101-102
Product quality, 20, 22

health and, 8
organizational effectiveness and, 101-103
Production, responsibility for, 96
Products
intangible, 22
services vs., 20
values and, 171
Profit, 20
employers and, 90-91, 103
values and, 171
Promotions, 69
equal employment opportunity and, 7
industriousness and, 96
mentors and, 98
Protecting response, 65-66

Q

Quality
award for, 101
organizational effectiveness and, 101-103
of work life, 9
See also Product quality
Quality improvement, 6, 101-103
Questions
semantic problems and, 120
teamwork and, 62-63

R

Race, 7
affirmative action and, 8
values and, 171
Reading, 126
Receiver, 118, 119, 136
Recognition
customer, 25
employee, 6, 69, 92
Recruiting
affirmative action and, 8
equal employment opportunity and, 7
Rehabilitation, 198
Relationship(s), 2-4
with customers, 2, 9, 29, 171
with employer, 3, 4, 9, 87-104
fear of, 195
trusting, 201-202
with yourself, 3-4, 155. *See also* Self-development
Religion, respecting, 56
Religious discrimination, 7
Rephrasing, 130
Respect, 56, 92
Responsibility, 6, 69
buildup of, 96
communication and, 130-132

employer expectations and, 95-96, 104
  of employers, 89, 103
  formal organization and, 130-132
Responsiveness, 200, 201
  customers and, 24-25
Retirement plans
  in 1950s, 6
  phased, 8
Rewards, 96
Risk, 200, 202
Rules, 59-62
  human rights and, 170
  values and concern for, 169-170
  written vs. unwritten, 60
  See also Policy
Rumors, 134-136
Russia, 57

S

Safety
  employers and, 103
  responsibility for, 95
  services and, 22
Salary, 7. *See also* Pay; Money
Sample-of-one judgment, 121
Satisfaction, 69
Self-confidence, 193
  fears and, 195
  positive self-image and, 194
Self-control, 6
Self-criticism, 197
Self-development, 4, 155-192
  brain dominance theory and, 164
  self-knowledge and, 162-164
  values and, 164-171
Self-direction, 6
Self-image, 156, 193
  criticism and, 197
  negative, 194
  physical health and, 197-198
  positive, 193, 194-202
  rating scale for, 157
  values and, 166, 168
Self-knowledge, 162-163
Self-talk, 197
Self-understanding, 4
Semantics, 119-120
Sender, 118, 119
Seniority system, 60-61
Service organizations, 20, 22
Services
  knowledge of, 31
  products and, 20, 22
  quality of, 101
  values and, 171
Sex discrimination, 7, 124

Sexist language, 124
Sexual harassment, 8
Shared decision making, 6
Sharing credit, 71
Short-term goals, 203
Sick leave, 63. *See also* Leave (of absence)
Skills. *See* Job skills
Small-group problem solving, 6
Smoking, 198
Spain, 58
Speaking, 126-127, 130
Sporting events, corporate, 197
Strategy, 8
Strengths, 194-195
Stress, 197, 198-199
Substance abuse, 8
Success, 8-9, 193-221
  characteristics of people who achieve, 199-201
  employers and, 90-91, 94, 96
  positive self-image and, 193, 194-202
Supervisors
  communication from, 132
  customers and, 33
  organization chart and, 130
  relationships with, 3
  See also Employers; Managers
Suppliers
  affirmative action and, 8
  employers and, 103

T

Team spirit, 9
Teamwork, 3, 55-86
  acceptance and, 56-59
  and asking questions, 62-63
  and "carrying your own weight," 62-65
  conflict management and, 65-68
  getting ahead and, 69-71
  rules and, 59-62
  See also Co-workers
Technical knowledge, 9
Telecommuting, 8
Terminations, 7
Territorial rights, 61
Time
  fear of investing, 195
  goals and, 204
Time/days off, 7, 8, 60
Title VII, 7
Titles, 123-124
Tobacco, 197
Tolerance, 66-68
Trade-offs, 205-206
Training
  in communication, 117

  equal employment opportunity and, 7
Transfers, 7
Trial and error, 158-159, 160
Trustworthiness, 94-95, 162, 199, 200-202
Turnover, 9

U

Unions, 60, 61
Uruguay, 58

V

Vacations, 60
Values, 164-171
  factors affecting, 166
  justice and, 168-171
  managing by, 171
Vendors, affirmative action and, 8
Voice mail, 136, 138

W

Weaknesses, 194-195
Wellness programs, 8
Western Electric experiment, 4-5, 6
Women
  affirmative action and, 8
  employment discrimination and, 6
  sexist language and, 124
Word-of-mouth advertising, 28-29
Words, 119-120
  emotionally loaded, 124, 125
  emotions and, 123-125
  positive vs. negative, 124, 125
  sexist, 124
Work
  and family issues, 8
  "hard" (industriousness), 96
  reasons for, 92
  secondary location for, 8
Work breaks, 63-64
  authoritarian managers and, 99
  seniority system and, 61
Work force, diverse, 8
Work schedules
  contract and, 60
  democratic managers and, 99
Working conditions
  employee expectations and, 92-93
  equal employment opportunity and, 7
  in 1950s, 6
Workplace, flexible, 7, 8
Writing, 126

Photo Credits

Chapter 1
Illustrations 1-2, 1-5, 1-6, 1-7: © 1997, PhotoDisk Inc.

Chapter 2
Illustrations 2-1C, 2-1D, 2-4B, Pg 41: © 1997, PhotoDisk, Inc.; Illustrations 2-1B, 2-3A, 2-4A, 2-5: Alan Brown/Photonics; Illustration 2-3B: © Jeff Greenberg

Chapter 3
Illustrations 3-1, 3-4, 3-5, 3-7, 3-8, 3-12, 3-13, 3-17A, 3-17C: © 1997, PhotoDisk, Inc.; Illustration 3-3: Alan Brown/Photonics

Chapter 4
Illustrations 4-2A, 4-2B, 4-6, 4-9, 4-10, 4-11: © 1997, PhotoDisk, Inc.; Illustrations 4-1, 4-7: Alan Brown/Photonics

Chapter 6
Illustrations 6-6, 6-11, 6-17: © 1997, PhotoDisk, Inc.

Chapter 7
Illustrations 7-1, 7-2, 7-4, 7-7, 7-9, 7-11: © 1997, PhotoDisk, Inc.